Cambridge Elements ☰

Elements in the Philosophy of Immanuel Kant
edited by
Desmond Hogan
Princeton University
Howard Williams
University of Cardiff
Allen Wood
Indiana University

THE ETHICAL COMMONWEALTH IN HISTORY

Peace-Making as the Moral Vocation of Humanity

Philip J. Rossi
Marquette University, Wisconsin

CAMBRIDGE
UNIVERSITY PRESS

CAMBRIDGE
UNIVERSITY PRESS

University Printing House, Cambridge CB2 8BS, United Kingdom

One Liberty Plaza, 20th Floor, New York, NY 10006, USA

477 Williamstown Road, Port Melbourne, VIC 3207, Australia

314–321, 3rd Floor, Plot 3, Splendor Forum, Jasola District Centre, New Delhi – 110025, India

79 Anson Road, #06–04/06, Singapore 079906

Cambridge University Press is part of the University of Cambridge.

It furthers the University's mission by disseminating knowledge in the pursuit of education, learning, and research at the highest international levels of excellence.

www.cambridge.org
Information on this title: www.cambridge.org/9781108438636
DOI: 10.1017/9781108529686

© Philip J. Rossi 2019

First published 2019

A catalogue record for this publication is available from the British Library.

ISBN 978-1-108-43863-6 Paperback
ISSN 2514-3824 (print)
ISSN 2397-9461 (online)

The Ethical Commonwealth in History

Peace-Making as the Moral Vocation of Humanity

Elements in the Philosophy of Immanuel Kant

DOI: 10.1017/9781108529686
First published online: July 2019

Philip J. Rossi
Marquette University, Wisconsin
Author for correspondence: Philip J. Rossi, philip.rossi@marquette.edu

Abstract: The "ethical commonwealth," the central social element in Immanuel Kant's account of religion, provides the Church, as "the moral people of God," with a role in establishing a cosmopolitan order of peace. This role functions within an interpretive realignment of Kant's critical project that articulates its central concern as anthropological: critically disciplined reason enables humanity to enact peace-making as its moral vocation in history. Within this context, politics and religion are not peripheral elements in the critical project. They are, instead, complementary social modalities in which humanity enacts its moral vocation to bring lasting peace among all peoples.

Keywords: peace, religion, highest good, cosmopolitanism, moral community

ISBNs: 9781108438636 (PB), 9781108529686 (OC)
ISSNs: 2397-9461 (online), 2514-3824 (print)

Contents

1 Introduction: Politics, Religion, and the Scope of Kant's Critical Project   1

2 Critique as Anthropology: The Duality of Human Reason in the World   11

3 Critique and Cosmopolitanism: The Anthropological Shaping of Religion and Politics   20

4 The Ethical Commonwealth: Social Imperative for Cosmopolitan Peace-Making   42

Bibliography   59

1 Introduction: Politics, Religion, and the Scope of Kant's Critical Project

Immanuel Kant (1724–1804) is generally placed among the most influential proponents of the European Enlightenment and its core values, such as human dignity, freedom of inquiry and expression, and individual moral autonomy. During most of the twentieth century, the prevailing interpretation of Kant's philosophy located the main line of inquiry in his enterprise for determining the scope and the limits of human reason – an enterprise he named a "critique" – principally within the field of academic philosophy known as epistemology. It was thus taken to be an effort to provide an account of how and what humans beings are capable of knowing truly and with certainty about the world and about themselves as participants in the world. This interpretation accordingly views the central outcome of Kant's inquiry, which he first sets forth in his monumental *Critique of Pure Reason* (1781; 2nd edition 1787), as a claim about the limits of human knowledge: genuine human knowledge is restricted to the field of objects that, inasmuch as they present themselves to our human senses under the conditions of space and time, can be represented by our cognitive capacities in accord with the necessarily connected conceptual patterns ("categories") that our reason provides us. In less technical terms, this claim means our human cognitive capacities can yield genuine knowledge only for those objects and principles that are part of a world of "matter and motion," i.e., the material world that is physically measurable in reference to space and time.

This claim about the limits of genuine human knowledge accordingly provides the basis upon which Kant then elaborates in subsequent writings a critical philosophy that radically undercuts the long-standing philosophical enterprise of "metaphysics." That enterprise sought to articulate a comprehensive conceptual account of all that exists, including whatever may exist in ways that "transcend" the physical world and thus stand "outside" the limiting conditions of space and time. Such efforts at metaphysics, which are traceable as far back as Plato, Aristotle, and other ancient Greek philosophers, were represented in Kant's time in the rationalist systems elaborated by thinkers such as Gottfried Leibniz, Christian Wolff, and Alexander Baumgarten. These rationalist systems of metaphysics also were proposed as the basis upon which one could reason philosophically to (at least a limited) knowledge of realities that stand beyond the limiting conditions of space and time, such as God, the immortal human soul with a capacity for freedom, and the basic principles of morality, such as good and justice. These rationalist systems of metaphysics thus served as one of the chief targets against which Kant directed his construction of a "critical" account of human knowing. In many versions of this account, Kant's critical philosophy heralded "the end of metaphysics," an intellectual program espoused by various philosophers in the nineteenth and twentieth centuries and that continues in the twenty-first.[1]

The rendition of Kant's philosophy I briefly elaborate here has been "standard" in the sense that it has frequently served as the narrative "backbone" of the account of Kant given in textbooks and lectures in university courses in "modern" philosophy, a period most often taken to comprise the span from René Descartes in the seventeenth century until Kant and (at least) some of his nineteenth-century successors.[2] A variety of elaborations and additions can be made to this basic narrative, many of which take account of the importance and influence of aspects of Kant's philosophy other than epistemology, most notably his writings on morality and ethics. Yet even those accounts may tread lightly when it comes to presenting the systemic and conceptual connections among all the topics that were of concern to Kant in the course of his elaboration of the critical project during the 1780s and 1790s. A particularly challenging connection to articulate adequately is the relationship between, on one hand, the writings in which Kant's account of the limits of human knowing are seen as undermining the claims of metaphysics and, on the other hand, the writings in which he articulates the moral demands that he takes reason to place in no uncertain way upon our human moral intention and agency. In the former, the concepts of human freedom, the soul, and God are treated, in view of the limits critical philosophy requires us to place on human knowledge, as extravagant illusions leading to seemingly insuperable contradictions ("antinomies");[3] in the latter, Kant sees the unconditional demand of moral duty (the "categorical imperative") that reason unmistakably places upon our conduct as providing a firm and indisputable basis upon which human reason may then confidently

---

[1] One good instance of what had become the interpretation representative of twentieth-century Kant scholarship, particularly in the Anglophone world, is W. H. Walsh's entry "Kant" in *The Encyclopedia of Philosophy*, ed. P. Edwards (New York: Macmillan Publishing & The Free Press, 1967), vol. 3, pp. 305–324. Another is the two-chapter treatment of Kant in J. Collins, *A History of Modern European Philosophy* (Milwaukee, WI: Bruce Publishing, 1954).

[2] For an incisive criticism of readings of Kant that place epistemology and the overcoming of metaphysics at its interpretive center, see S. Neiman, "Meaning and Metaphysics," in *Teaching New Histories of Philosophy*, ed. J. B. Schneewind (Princeton, NJ: University Center for Human Values, 2004), pp. 29–50.

[3] Kant presents a vivid image of the limitations of "understanding," the term he uses to designate human cognitive capacities, at CPR A235-236/B294-295: "We have now not only traveled through the land of pure understanding, and carefully inspected each part of it, but we have also surveyed it, and determined the place for each thing in it. But this land is an island, and enclosed in unalterable boundaries by nature itself. It is the land of truth (a charming name), surrounded by a broad and stormy ocean, the true seat of illusion, where many a fog bank and rapidly melting iceberg pretend to be new lands and, ceaselessly deceiving with empty hopes the voyager looking around for new discoveries, entwine him in adventures from which he can never escape and yet also never bring to an end."

affirm what he terms the "practical reality" of the "transcendental ideas" of human freedom, the soul, and God.[4] Kant's account of morality and its implications thus seems to restore the very objects, i.e., human freedom, the soul, and God, that his critique of metaphysics had proposed were beyond the reach of our human knowing – a criticism Kant himself encountered during his lifetime.[5]

One particularly influential form of this "backbone" narrative has taken the lasting philosophical significance of Kant's work to lie in the way in which his critical articulation of the limits of human knowing has become the wrecking ball that demolishes not just the rationalist metaphysics of his day but also the entire enterprise of Western speculative metaphysics. A number of problems occur with this version of the narrative, not the least of which is that Kant himself continues to use the term "metaphysics" to designate certain portions of his critical project. A notable instance is *The Metaphysics of Morals* (1797), among the last of the book-length works published during Kant's lifetime as part of the critical project. Enough other evidence certainly exists for Kant's continuing use of the term "metaphysics" to indicate that, whatever else the critical project had as its purpose, it was *not* to demolish metaphysics root and branch.[6] It was rather to reform metaphysics into an enterprise more modest in scale, a scale appropriate to one of the fundamental aims of Kant's project: to give appropriate recognition to the limited, finite character of human reason and its use, particularly in view of a human tendency to overstep those finite limits.[7]

---

[4] The main textual locus for Kant's presentation of the Antinomies of Reason is in the *Critique of Pure Reason* (CPR) A405/B432-A567/B595. A major statement of his argument for affirming the "practical reality" of human freedom, the immortality of the human soul, and God is found in the *Critique of Practical Reason* (CPrR), 5:113–158. C. J. Insole, *The Intolerable God: Kant's Theological Journey* (Grand Rapids, MI: William B. Eerdmans, 2016) provides a provocative account of the underlying tensions between human freedom and God that are represented in both Kant's articulation of the antinomies and his ongoing attempts to resolve this tension.

[5] On the ambiguities in Kant's views and arguments O. O'Neil remarks, "Many of his readers have thought that he eventually endorses the substantial view of the self that he ostensibly repudiates, and that his ethical writings return to the transcendental theology and metaphysics that he so convincingly put into question in earlier works" ("Reason and Politics in the Kantian Enterprise," in *Constructions of Reason* [Cambridge: Cambridge University Press, 1989], p. 4).

[6] More than a decade before *The Metaphysics of Morals*, Kant published the *Groundwork of the Metaphysics of Morals* (G) and *Metaphysical Foundations of Natural Science* (MFNS) in 1784 and 1785, respectively; in the period between the publication of these three works, he began preparing a treatise for submission to an essay contest, announced in 1790, that was sponsored by the Royal Academy of Berlin on the question "What real progress has metaphysics made in Germany since the time of Wolff and Leibniz?" Kant's treatise, which remained incomplete and was not submitted for the second and final announced deadline of June 1795, was published after Kant's death in its fragmentary form by his friend Friedrich Theodor Rink in 1804 (AA 20:259–351).

[7] O'Neill, in the four essays that constitute Part I of *Constructions of Reason*, offers a number of astute observations on the role that the recognition of the finitude of reason plays in shaping Kant's critical project. She offers the image of "the cottage of Immanuel Kant" ("Reason and Politics in the Kantian Enterprise," p. 11) to portray the self-disciplined scope of Kant's project in

Accounts of Kant's enterprise that take the cognitive delegitimation of metaphysics to be its most significant result (and perhaps even its intended outcome), however, provide little positive scope for then connecting this reading of its main trajectory with the larger constructive and systemic expectations that Kant articulates for his enterprise within its very advocacy of a more "modest" metaphysics. Kant sees the critically disciplined use of reason – one that recognizes both the importance and the limitations of the deeply embedded human "disposition" to metaphysics – as continuing to have a fundamental and necessary bearing upon the full range of human inquiry and activity.[8] These include, but are not limited to, ethics, history, religion, politics, anthropology, aesthetics, education, and culture, all of which Kant indicates have integral connections with the project of constructing a critical philosophy. A number of places in Kant's critical writings indicate that, in addition to the fundamental importance that the enterprise of critique has for reason's governance of human moral activity and ethical inquiry, two other fields of human activity for which a critique of reason is of crucial significance for reason to exercise proper governance are religion and politics.[9] This suggests that an account of the overall trajectory of Kant's project of critique needs both to identify the place that these forms of human activity and inquiry have within the larger critical enterprise, and to characterize how their specific functions within that enterprise bear upon one another.

It is thus within the context of rendering the scope of Kant's critical enterprise as having a horizon more encompassing than that provided by the task of overcoming, by dint of epistemic rigor, the rationalist school metaphysics of his age, that this Element articulates an account of the role that his philosophy of religion and his political philosophy play within that enterprise. It does so by identifying the basis from which the fundamental trajectory of the critical project – i.e., its central focus on the anthropological questions of what it is and what it means to be human – squarely places both forms of inquiry, and the human activities from which they arise, within the ambit of that project; this anthropological focus, moreover, also locates them in a way that shows the integral link they have to one another as elements of Kant's critical enterprise.

---

striking contrast to the raising of grandiose conceptual "towers" characteristic of rationalist system building.

[8] Kant discusses metaphysics as "disposition" in the concluding sections of the *Prolegomena to Any Future Metaphysics* (P 4:250–272).

[9] Kant's 1784 essay "Idea for a Universal History with a Cosmopolitan Aim" (IUH) can be considered a programmatic statement of the task that humanity as a species is called upon to undertake with respect to the end that "nature" bestows on it, as human reason becomes critically self-disciplined in the course of history in the development of human society.

In the background of this question about the connections linking these two particular elements within Kant's critical project is a larger one that has long vexed scholars and students of Kant's work: to what extent does Kant succeed in articulating and justifying his oft-made claim – and his even more frequently operative presupposition – that it is one and the same finite reason that humanity employs both for understanding the natural workings of the world ("theory") and for living morally in that world ("practice")?[10] One telling sign that Kant was not all that successful in making a convincing case for the unity of reason among those who have placed themselves among his philosophical followers is that there seems to be little expectation in the philosophical community that being a "Kantian" moral philosopher then commits one also to being "Kantian" in, for instance, one's epistemology, philosophical anthropology, metaphysics, or philosophy of religion – or vice versa. Given that the jury is still out – and is likely to remain out for a long time – on the question of the adequacy of Kant's treatment of the unity of reason, this Element does not attempt to resolve this larger question as it sets forth an account of the more specific relationship between Kant's philosophy of religion and his political philosophy. Note, however, that its treatment of this specific relationship works from an inter-pretive presupposition that seeks to respect Kant's operative commitment to the unity of reason and to identify the elements in his treatment of religion and of politics from a critical standpoint on which such unity has a bearing.

Against the background of a long-standing interpretive preoccupation with the cognitive strictures that Kant's critique places upon metaphysical inquiry, it is hardly surprising that his writings on religion and politics have often been treated in relative independence from claims that bear upon the unity of critical reason. One consequence of this has been that the main interpretive issues that arise in reading these texts on religion and politics are often not framed from a perspective attending to what their roles might be within his larger critical enterprise. Instead, the interpretive focus turns to issues that, as important as they may be in their own right, are not always pertinent to what, as I argue, Kant sees as the overriding concern that gives shape to his critical writings and to the bearing that concern has upon his claims about the unity of human finite reason. This concern is not, as the standard interpretation often has it, to limit – if not to eliminate – human claims to possess metaphysical knowledge. It is, instead, a

---

[10] See S. Neiman, *The Unity of Reason: Re-reading Kant* (Oxford: Oxford University Press, 1994) for a particularly insightful account of what is philosophically at stake in Kant's commitment to the unity of reason as a fundamental orientation for his critical enterprise. She offers a less technical account of that commitment in *Evil in Modern Thought: An Alternative History of Philosophy* (Princeton, NJ: Princeton University Press, 2002), where she argues that for Kant, "ethics and metaphysics are not accidentally connected" (p. 327).

far more encompassing concern for understanding our humanity and its relation to the world in which we dwell and act. This concern, with roots stretching back to the earliest origins of Western philosophy, makes Kant's critical project one that is at root anthropological: it seeks to enable us to articulate, first of all, a sound understanding (which is also constitutively a *self*-understanding) of what makes "us" – embodied, finite knowers and agents who are integrally part of a material world that works in accord with laws of natural necessity – distinctively "human." The articulation of such a sound self-understanding of our humanity, moreover, is not simply a *descriptive* ("theoretical") achievement telling us what "kind" of being we are in relation to other "kinds" in the world. Such a critical self-understanding of our humanity also provides a frame of reference from which we can then articulate the *normative* ("practical") points of reference that our humanity enjoins upon us for directing our ways of living in this world with one another in a human community.

One shorthand way to characterize this central concern informing Kant's critical enterprise is that it aims to make us self-aware of "the human place in the cosmos" as the locus from which reason enjoins upon us to live out a distinctively human "moral vocation": this vocation is to make "the highest good in the world" possible through the exercise of our human reason. When viewed from this anthropological framework, which bids humanity to participate in the achievement of the highest good in the world, Kant's writings on religion and on politics can be seen as both integrally a part of the critical project and closely connected to each other. Their connection with one another has its basis in how they each serve as mutually supportive elements of the social and historical dimensions of the critical project: they have complementary roles for what Kant sees as the social and historical unfolding and accomplishment of humanity's moral vocation in the world through the exercise of reason. Both their connection with one another and their role in the critical project are specified by their serving as interrelated but distinguishable elements for the social and historical enactment of what Kant envisions as a cosmopolitan human community.

On Kant's account, the historical instantiation of such a community provides the locus for humanity to work together to provide the moral and political conditions for making "the highest good in the world" concretely possible. Chief among these conditions is the construction of a cosmopolitan world political order for establishing an enduring peace among nations; in the historical construction of that order, moreover, politics and religion have complementary roles in setting the social conditions that will make enduring peace possible. In consequence, the larger anthropological trajectory of the critical project, which aims toward articulating the distinctive place of humanity in the cosmos, may be said to have as one of its important outcomes the articulation and the legitimation of human efforts to enact peace-making on a global scale. Such efforts constitute a concrete marker for what Kant's critical philosophy assigns as the moral vocation of humanity in history and in these efforts, religion and politics each play an important role in the formation of the social dynamics constitutive of enduring peace.[11]

My argument proceeds in three stages. The first stage, "Kant's Critique as Anthropology: The Duality of Human Reason in the World," proposes some of the key considerations that indicate that there are good reasons, based on Kant's texts, for enlarging the fundamental scope of the critical project beyond the epistemological and metaphysical concerns that have often preoccupied Kant's interpreters. This expanded scope is an anthropological one; it arises from Kant's efforts to articulate and resolve what he takes to be a fundamental duality at the core of our humanity. At one level, this duality is experiential: we are aware of being inextricably part of a cosmos governed in accord with universal physical laws of its material nature and, at the same time, also inextricably participants in a world of human interaction whose social and historical trajectory requires governance by human agents through the mutual exercise of their moral freedom. At another level, the duality is one that we can articulate reflectively in terms of the conceptual contrast between the necessary operations of "nature" and the autonomy of (human) "freedom." The locus of that tension – both experiential and reflective – lies within humanity itself, and Kant's critical project sees this polarity as arguably irresolvable, that is, as long as human reason does not subject itself to the self-limiting discipline he terms "critique." The urgency in resolving this duality provides the critical project with its core intellectual and moral energy: Kant takes this polarity between nature and freedom, as humanity both experiences it and reflexively engages it in the exercise of reason, to constitute the historical and social locus in which humanity is called upon to enact its moral vocation to serve as the very juncture that *enacts nature and freedom into unity.* The unity of reason thus is not a predetermined given; it is, instead, a project for human enactment, a project that extends throughout the course of human history.

Working from the presupposition that such an anthropological turn provides a sound interpretive background for Kant's critical enterprise, the second stage, "Critique and Cosmopolitanism: The Anthropological Shaping of Religion and Politics," considers key elements in, respectively, Kant's philosophy of religion

---

[11] See A. W. Wood, *Kant's Ethical Thought* (Cambridge: Cambridge University Press, 1999), chapter 9, "The Historical Vocation of Humanity," pp. 283–320, for an account of Kant's larger perspective on the circumstances that call upon humanity to consider its moral responsibility to be one that pertains to it as a species.

and his political philosophy. These elements have often been controverted, but, as I argue, when these controversies are reexamined with an eye toward the larger anthropological trajectory of the critical project, they provide pointers toward the complementary roles that critically shaped politics and religion have in that project: they function as central historical and social modalities through which humanity enacts its moral vocation.

In the case of religion, I situate Kant's account along an anthropological trajectory that, even as it still attends to epistemic issues arising from specifically Christian doctrines, focuses on a dimension of religion that is more fundamental for its role in the critical enterprise than is doctrinal exactness. This dimension consists in the role that religion, in the modality of "hope," plays in humanity's moral vocation, as the juncture of nature and freedom, to enact "the highest good in the world" as "the ultimate end" of human reason.[12] Kant takes "hope" as marking the function of religion as it is construed "within the boundaries of mere reason": hope enables humanity to envision the concrete contours of "the moral world" that is to be enacted in history in virtue of the unitary workings of critically disciplined human reason. Hope functions by envisioning "the world as it would be if it were in conformity with all moral laws" (CPR A808/B836) in the context of the distinctive social and historical conditions that are a central part of humanity's unique status as an embodied and finite rational species. Hope enables the envisioning of such a world in the form of an "ethical commonwealth" that enacts the social dynamics of a thoroughgoing mutual respect of one another's freedom.[13]

It is of crucial importance for understanding Kant's articulation of hope to recognize that, from the earliest stages of the critical project, he takes the ambit of the hope that reason critically enables us to hold to be one that is a thoroughly social one: hope bears upon our humanity not simply individually – as would be the case if its only focus were on the happiness proper just to my individual virtue – but also in and through our relationality to one another in a moral community constituted in the recognition and the exercise of our mutual freedom.[14] The social images he uses consistently throughout the critical project ("kingdom of grace," "kingdom of ends") offer one striking marker of

---

[12] "The Canon of Pure Reason," First Section and Second Section (CPR A797/B825-A819/847) provides an initial textual locus for Kant's account of the "end" of human reason. See F. C. Beiser, "Moral Faith and the Highest Good," in *The Cambridge Companion to Kant and Modern Philosophy*, ed. P. Guyer (Cambridge: Cambridge University Press, 2006), pp. 588–629, for the bearing of the highest good upon the end of human reason.

[13] See *Religion within the Boundaries of Mere Reason*, Part III (Rel. 6:93–147) for Kant's exposition of the "ethical commonwealth."

[14] See P. J. Rossi, SJ, *The Social Authority of Reason: Kant's Critique, Radical Evil and the Destiny of Humankind* (Albany: State University of New York Press, 2005) for an account of the social character of hope and its role in Kant's critical project.

this. The image that he uses in *Religion*, the "ethical commonwealth," is of particular significance since it serves as an apt bridge for linking what Kant recognizes as the distinctively moral, political, and religious "inflections" of human community in service of concrete human efforts to participate in the enactment of the highest good.

In politics, Kant's proposal for the establishment of an international order to bring about a state of enduring peace – which is arguably the element of his political philosophy that has shown remarkable staying power as a point of reference for efforts to establish transnational rules and structures to curb armed conflict – is similarly repositioned along an anthropological trajectory. This trajectory is similarly indexed to the enactment of the highest good in the world as "the ultimate end" of human reason in a thoroughly social form. Two elements in Kant's proposal are of particular importance for this anthropological repositioning. One is that Kant's identification of the establishment of such an international order for enduring peace as "the highest political good" brings the project of perpetual peace into his wider articulation of the ends of reason and the central place these ends hold in the moral vocation of humanity. The second is that this project is itself part of Kant's larger envisioning of a cosmopolitan world order as a fundamental social mode for the instantiation of the highest good in the world. From the anthropological trajectory of the critical project Kant's cosmopolitanism can be understood as an overarching articulation of the distinctive social and historical vocation that is fitting to humanity's unique status as an embodied and finite rational species. In virtue of this status, humanity lives out its vocation as a species within the concrete historical workings of society and culture; it does so by exercising its moral freedom to bring about the individual and social conditions that conjointly make historical progress toward attaining "the highest good" possible. Chief among the social conditions for historical progress toward such good is one that emerges from the dynamics of human political activity and whose establishment concretely takes a political form: the constructing of a cosmopolitan world political order for establishing an enduring peace among nations.

The argument that this second stage makes on behalf of the bearing both religion and politics have upon the human enactment of the ultimate end of reason thus also indicates their role in Kant's discussions of the overarching aim of the critical enterprise. These discussions do not just point to the large anthropological question – What is humanity? – at the heart of the critical enterprise. They also frame that question in terms that locate its religious dimension and its political dimension in reference to the task of enacting the highest good in the world. A cosmopolitan world order for enduring peace and the ethical commonwealth thus provide, respectively, the political and the religious "inflections" in which human reason articulates the social shape of the highest good in the world as the human enactment of the ultimate end of its finite reason.[15]

The third and final stage, "The Ethical Commonwealth: Social Imperative for Cosmopolitan Peace-Making," of this Element's argument for the integral connection that Kant makes between religion and politics focuses on the role that "hope," a key element in his account of religion, plays in that connection. Hope provides a horizon from which to extend Kant's account of the establishment of an international cosmopolitan order for enduring peace beyond the ambit of the political, the field for external and enforceable regulation of the conduct of nations. I argue that this extension can be made in terms of his account of the dynamics of the ethical commonwealth, the central social element of his account of critically disciplined religion. These dynamics serve as the locus within which "the true Church," as "the moral people of God," can play a role in the historical establishment of peace among the peoples of the world (Rel. 6:98–102, 115–124).

The extension I am proposing here thus arises on the basis of construing the (political) enactment of a cosmopolitan order of lasting peace as enabled through the exercise of human freedom that has been socially empowered for peace-making. Social empowerment arises from the hope for effective human participation in the enactment of the highest good in the world, the hope that is the focus of the (religious) dynamism of the mutuality of freedom constitutive of the ethical commonwealth. This social empowerment for peace-making thus serves as the locus within which religion and politics play complementary roles in the concrete historical attainment of the cosmopolitan end of human reason that is envisioned in the critical project: a social empowerment for peace-making arises from the perspective of the hope that is the *religious* inflection of the *moral* dynamism of the ethical commonwealth.

Relative to the overall anthropological trajectory of the critical project, a complementary religious rendering can be appropriately given to the establishment of a cosmopolitan world order for peace that Kant envisions in political terms in "Perpetual Peace" (1795). The attainment of this highest political good for humanity can be rendered religiously as the social and historical instantiation of empowerment of the moral freedom made possible by the mutual respect constitutive of the social dynamics of the ethical

---

[15] See Wood, *Kant's Ethical Thought*, pp. 193–207, for a brief account of the development of Kant's own understanding of anthropology and its role in his critical project. For more extensive treatments, see H. L. Wilson, *Kant's Pragmatic Anthropology: Its Origin, Meaning, and Critical Significance* (Albany: State University of New York Press, 2006) and J. H. Zammito, *Kant, Herder, and the Birth of Anthropology* (Chicago: University of Chicago Press, 2002).

commonwealth. Such empowerment provides humanity with a horizon of hope from which to envision possibilities for effectively overcoming the concrete forms of human social divisiveness that lie at the root of war and thereby creating conditions for the establishment of enduring peace.[16] This empowerment – which Kant sees modeled in religious terms by the life and death of Jesus that "most strikingly displays the contrast between the children of heaven and the bondage of a mere son of earth" (Rel. 6:82) – makes it possible to consider the efforts of human freedom exercised on behalf of a cosmopolitan world order for peace as also appropriately rendered religiously as a fundamental element for human participation in the (moral) work of God, which is the work of bringing about and sustaining peace.

2 Critique as Anthropology: The Duality of Human Reason in the World

Here I set forth the first stage of the argument for the integral connection between religion and politics in Kant's critical project. I begin with a brief overview of the philosophical context in which Kant undertook this project that serves to identify elements that played a role in bringing to the fore the question of human knowing as the primary frame of reference for subsequent interpretations of his work. Against this backdrop, I examine some key considerations in Kant's texts indicating that, at work in his efforts to insure the certitude and validity of human knowing against strong currents of cultural and philosophical skepticism, is a more fundamental concern. The concern is anthropological, focused on understanding what it means to be human in the finite conditions and circumstances that constitute us and the world in which we dwell with one another.

Central to this stage of the argument is a discussion indicating how this anthropological trajectory arises from Kant's efforts to articulate and resolve a fundamental duality between "nature" and "freedom" that stands at the core of our experience and our reflective self-understanding of our human dwelling in the world. The outcome of Kant's efforts to resolve this duality indicates that humanity is itself the crucial juncture upon which nature and freedom converge. In consequence, the resolution of this duality is a distinctively human task, one that Kant construes as humanity's moral vocation. This vocation is one humanity is called upon to live within the finite conditions of both the determinate natural causality of the material world and the concrete historical workings of

---

[16] For one articulation of the bearing that a theological perspective could have upon the cosmopolitan project of constructing an order for lasting peace, see P. J. Rossi, SJ, "Models of God and Just War Theory," in *Models of God and Alternative Ultimate Realities*, ed. A. Kasher and J. Diller (Dordrecht: Springer Verlag, 2013), pp. 991–1000.

society and culture as arenas for the exercise of human freedom. In concrete terms, this vocation enjoins humanity to exercise its moral freedom to bring about the individual and social conditions that conjointly make historical progress toward attaining the highest good in the world possible.

Immanuel Kant published his three *Critiques* in the years 1781–1790. During that same period, and well into the decade of the 1790s, he produced what are arguably the most significant of his writings on religion, politics, history, and human culture.[17] None of these works was on the monumental scale of the *Critique of Pure Reason*, the first work of his critical project; neither did they offer accounts comparable in scope to the comprehensive systemic claims that Kant made in the set of *Critiques*, claims made with the intent of articulating and legitimating the proper uses of human finite reason in its intertwined activities of knowing the world, governing conduct morally, and making judgments of beauty and purpose. Kant raises fundamental questions about the scope and limits of human knowledge at the outset of the first *Critique* and insistently purses them throughout its more than 800 pages. His responses to these questions and the consequences these have for the full range of the uses of human finite reason provide the context from which he then engages the two other activities of reason he sees as correlatively fundamental to that of knowing: reason as it functions in governing our conduct morally, the focus of the *Critique of Practical Reason*, and reason as it functions in our making judgments of beauty and purpose, the focus of the *Critique of the Power of Judgment*. Against this background, it is hardly surprising that the other writings Kant produced during this period, in which he continued to elaborate his critical philosophy while also responding to the friendly and the hostile criticism it evoked, have been most often read and understood from a perspective that gives interpretive primacy to the fundamental questions about human knowing from which he set the initial trajectory of critique.

From this perspective, the three *Critiques* are taken to articulate Kant's comprehensive response to what had become in the course of the eighteenth century a chronically troubling crisis over the underpinnings and the certainty of human knowledge. This crisis had earlier taken a decisive turn in the efforts of René Descartes to respond to the radical skepticism within the intellectual

---

[17] Among the most significant of these are "Idea for a Universal History with a Cosmopolitan Aim" (1784); "An Answer to the Question: What Is Enlightenment?" (1784); "What Does It Mean to Orient Oneself in Thinking?" (1786); "On the Common Saying: That May Be Correct in Theory But It Is of No Use in Practice" (1793); *Religion within the Boundaries of Mere Reason* (1793); "Toward Perpetual Peace" (1795); *The Metaphysics of Morals* (1797); "An Old Question Raised Again: Is the Human Race Constantly Progressing?" (1798).

culture of post-Reformation Europe. He did so by locating the underpinnings of knowledge in the self-enclosed *cogito* ("I think, therefore I am") of the individual human subject as it proceeds methodically from certainty of its own existence as "a thinking thing" to an overcoming of the most radical doubt about the reality of God and the external world by a method of reasoning in accord with rules modeled on the rigor of geometrical logic. Neither Descartes's efforts, however, nor the efforts of other thinkers who followed various currents in his wake, fully resolved the crisis. In fact, the crisis deepened during the following century and a half, particularly in the face of the calmly articulated skeptical arguments proposed by David Hume to undercut the intelligibility of taking an examination of the contents of the consciousness of a stable "self" to be sufficient as a firm foundation for human knowledge.[18]

There can be little dispute that Kant takes the task of addressing questions about the manner and reliability of human knowing, as well as about the dynamics of the knowing human subject, to constitute central elements for the philosophical undertaking to which he gives the name "critique." From this stance, Kant's critical philosophy is an extended exercise in epistemology, the philosophy of knowledge, and, in keeping with "the turn to the subject" that Descartes made the basis for a philosophical resolution of the quest for human cognitive certainty, is a project focused on the individual knower as the prime locus of human cognitive subjectivity.[19]

In recent decades, however, studies of Kant's philosophy have proposed that this focus on the individual human subject as its fundamental point of reference may be too constricted to do justice to the central ambitions of Kant's philosophical project, particularly when it provides the sole lens through which to read the whole body of Kant's texts.[20] These works have explored possibilities of a more expansive understanding of Kant's works, ones that offer what might be considered, in contrast to the close-in focus on questions of the adequacy of human knowledge, a wide-angle, panoramic lens on the scope and method of the enterprise of critique. The view from this lens seeks to encompass the multifaceted human engagements with the world that, on Kant's account, serve as the loci in which human reason empowers our

---

[18] Hume offers such arguments in *A Treatise of Human Nature* (1738–1740), ed. L. A. Selby-Bigge (Oxford: Clarendon Press, 1888 rpt. 1968) Book 1, Part IV. VI "Of Personal Identity," pp. 251–263.

[19] It may be of some significance for gaining a historical perspective on this interpretive stance on Kant's work that the English-language term "epistemology," which has become the standard designation for the philosophy of knowledge, is a nineteenth-century coinage, traceable to Scottish philosopher James F. Ferrier (1808–1864). The *Oxford English Dictionary* lists its first use in *The Eclectic Magazine*, November 1847, and cites Ferrier's use of the term in *Institutes of Metaphysic: The Theory of Knowing and Being* (1854).

[20] See Neiman, "Meaning and Metaphysics," pp. 29–50.

activities of cognitive inquiry, moral governance of action, and aesthetic and purposive judgments.[21]

Seen from this more expansive focus, the central concern driving Kant's critical work may no longer be considered simply that of justifying human knowing. That concern may now be located as part of a larger project: an anthropological one that aims to understand how we are constituted as properly and distinctively human, *both* in and by all the activities we govern by our reason, *and* also by being an integral part of a material world governed by principles of nature.[22] Kant's enterprise of critique thus is concerned not only to articulate and to legitimate the scope of human knowing in the face of skeptical attacks but more fundamentally also to understand the shape and the structure of all the interrelated activities of our finite reason as they function as central to what constitutes us as human in the cosmos in which we dwell.

From this anthropological focus, the aim of Kant's critical philosophy is then not merely to resolve the crisis of human knowing in European philosophy that Descartes's works helped to precipitate in the mid-seventeenth century. It has a more expansive scope, one from which Kant can address the question of what constitutes us as human by framing it in reference to the distinctive status that he sees conferred upon humanity by the possession and exercise of human reason in its multiple functions. It is a status that Kant sees arising from a duality fundamental to humanity's placement in the world as an embodied and finite rational species and the consequences of this placement for the exercise of our finite reason.

On Kant's account, this duality presents itself to us as the twofold manner in which we must perforce engage the world, both as knowers and as moral agents,

---

[21] A long-standing focus on the *Groundwork of the Metaphysics of Moral* as the touchstone of Kant's moral philosophy had already placed some countervailing weight against the interpretive thrust to read his larger project in predominantly epistemological terms. Taking that text, however, as the key to Kant's ethics misses important developments he makes in his subsequent treatments of reason in its moral use, as Allen Wood has noted in his essay "The Final Form of Kant's Practical Philosophy." Of at least equal importance, moreover, is the fact that even though attention to *Groundwork* amplifies the interpretive frame of the critical philosophy into the ethical, it does so from the vantage point of a "thin" anthropology in which human moral agency is construed only in formal terms. It thus does not fully engage the role that such agency has for the concrete historical/cultural/social attainment of the end of reason that is proper to humanity as a species.

[22] Central to many of these rereadings of Kant is attention to the social and relational dimensions of Kant's account of human agency. A notable precursor for this line of interpretation is L. Goldmann, *Immanuel Kant*, Robert Black (trans.), London: NLB 1971 (French: *La communauté humaine et l'univers chez Kant*, 1948; German: *Mensch, Gemeinschaft und Welt in der Philosophie Immanuel Kants*, 1945). Other commentators who have since articulated this social dimension include Alix Cohen, Sharon Anderson Gold, Frederick Beiser, James DiCenso, Robert Louden, Susan Neiman, Philip J. Rossi, Roger Sullivan, Howard Williams, Holly Wilson, and Allen Wood.

in the use of our reason. On one side, which Kant designates "theoretical," reason enables and impels us to "think" the world: reason drives and serves our efforts to understand comprehensively the workings of the material world, including ourselves as thoroughly part of that world. Reason does this as a capacity by which we articulate the rules (concepts) and the systemic interconnection of those concepts (laws) as principles for the intelligible ordering of the workings of the world and of the interaction of all that is in the world. On the other side, which Kant designates "practical," reason impels and enables us to determine ourselves as moral agents in the world of human interaction. The world thus presents itself not just as a field for understanding (theoretically) the principles ordering its material working but also as a field for interaction (practice) that originates from the distinctively human moral self-governance of freedom that Kant calls "autonomy."

On Kant's account, this duality of the exercise of human reason is a marker of the fundamental duality of a humanity that at once dwells in a cosmos governed in accord with the necessary workings of universal physical laws and in a world of human interaction whose social and historical trajectory takes concrete shape under the governance of autonomous human agents. The cosmos of material nature and universal physical laws thus provides the field for the theoretical use of human reason, while the world of human interaction, whose social and historical trajectory is shaped by the moral freedom of human agents, constitutes the field for the practical use of human reason. A fundamental point of textual reference for Kant's articulation and exploration of this duality – but by no means the only one – is located in his extensive treatment of the "Third Antinomy" in the *Critique of Pure Reason* and his commentary on its resolution (CPR A444/B472-A451/B479; A462/B490-A476/B504; A532/B560-A558/B586). There he presents this duality as one that pits the causality of nature and the causality of freedom in dialectical tension with one another. The crucial role that this tension between nature and freedom plays in the unfolding of the critical enterprise is significantly underscored by Kant's later observations in the preface to the work that offers a second installment on the critical project, *Critique of Practical Reason* (1788). At the very outset of this text, he notes that the aim of the second *Critique*, i.e., showing "*that there is pure practical reason*," will also show that "transcendental freedom is also established" (CPrR 5:3) – a point that he then directly references to the duality of nature and freedom articulated in the third antinomy of the first *Critique*. He specifically observes that, in the second *Critique*, freedom is established "in that absolute sense in which speculative reason needed it, in its use of the concept of causality, in order to rescue it from the antinomy into which it inevitably fails when it wants to think the *unconditioned* in the series of causal connection" (CPrR 5:3).

The systematic importance of establishing this concept of freedom is further emphasized in the next paragraph by Kant's claim that "the concept of freedom, insofar as its reality is proved by an apodictic law of practical reason constitutes the *keystone* of the whole structure of pure reason, even of speculative reason" (CPrR 5:3–4). These remarks on the systemic importance that the relationship between nature and freedom has for the critical project, though phrased in abstract terms at the outset of the second *Critique*, significantly resonate with the concrete image Kant employs at the end of this work to evoke how human beings reflectively understand themselves as standing in a fundamental duality. The duality consists in the relation we have, on one hand, to the world of nature that (outwardly) presents itself to our senses and, on the other hand, to the world of human moral interaction that takes shape through the inner determinations of our freedom. The image Kant uses, moreover, points to the evocative power each relation has with respect to our human reflective self-understanding: "Two things fill the mind with ever new and increasing admiration and reverence, the more often and more steadily one reflects on them: *the starry heavens above me and the moral law within me*" (CPrR 5:161).[23]

These are two of the significantly placed passages from Kant's writings that suggest a particularly appropriate way to characterize the anthropological trajectory of the critical project: it is a trajectory that lies along coordinates locating *humanity itself as the crucial juncture upon which nature and freedom converge*. On this view, Kant's critical enterprise may then be understood as an effort to articulate, by examining the structures and operations of human reason, the distinctive place humanity thereby occupies in the cosmos: humanity itself – and in particular the finite reason that humanity is called up to exercise in the world – constitutes the central locus upon which and in which nature and freedom converge. Within this anthropological trajectory, questions about the underpinnings and reliability of human knowing as it bears upon the workings of nature are quite significant; they do not, however, constitute the sole or final focus of Kant's efforts to articulate, in a context marked by an expanding scientific knowledge of the world and a growing reflective awareness of the human dynamics of history and society, what it means to be human. Kant's efforts to engage this anthropological question thus may be taken (unsurprisingly) to be evocative of a larger line of inquiry beyond the epistemological one dominant for much of modernity, a line of inquiry that goes back to the very origins of Western philosophy: the Delphic

---

[23] Neiman, *Evil in Modern Thought*, provides a thoughtful account of the phenomenological contours of this duality in a section titled "Kant: Divided Wisdom," pp. 57–84.

inscription "know thyself" that once served to propel Socrates's practice of inquiry in Athens.[24]

This injunction gets writ large more than two millennia later in and for Kant's critical project. For Kant, this injunction now bears upon the self-knowledge of humanity not only as individuals but also as a whole, a humanity that he, as an advocate of enlightenment, sees as ready to take up the task of coming of age, a task in which the self-reflective enterprise of critique has an important role.[25] In consequence of this ambition of Kant's project, the Delphic injunction no longer bears just upon self-knowledge of one's own soul but also upon the self-knowledge of a humanity that has become more reflectively aware of its distinctive status and role both in the material cosmos and in the sociocultural dynamics of human history. It is no longer an injunction just for an individual soul that strives, in its Platonic guise, to ascend from the shadows playing upon the wall of the Cave to reach full illumination in light of the Good or, in its Aristotelian guise, to secure, in the manner of the unmoved divine first substance, the inner and outer conditions for self-sufficient philosophical contemplation of first principles. It has become an injunction that, in the critical form Kant gives to it, now bears upon humanity as a species, not just individually; it indicates that there is *an ineradicable social dimension to the human self-knowledge that emerges from critique.* Such socially attentive self-knowledge now also stands included in the task that reason calls upon humanity to undertake along a trajectory that takes concrete historical shape through the exercise of human moral freedom.

This account of humanity's distinctive moral vocation as the juncture of nature and freedom thus serves to enlarge the interpretive frame for Kant's critical enterprise into an anthropological one. Within this frame, humanity serves as the juncture of nature and freedom to the extent that it recognizes and lives in accord with the limits and the ends that "critique" self-reflectively places upon the use of finite reason as it governs human theoretical and practical engagement with the cosmos. The enterprise of critique thus plays a key role in reason's governance of our human engagement with the cosmos: critique, on Kant's account, is constituted by humanity's free undertaking of the

---

[24] Kant hints at this lineage in a remark he makes in "The Architectonic of Pure Reason": "The former [i.e., the final end of reason] is nothing other than the entire vocation of human beings and the philosophy of it is called moral philosophy. On account of the preeminence which moral philosophy had over all applications of reason, the ancients understood by the name of 'philosopher' first and foremost the moralist and even the outer appearance of self-control through reason still suffices today for calling someone a philosopher after a certain analogy in spite of his limited knowledge" (CPR A840/B868).

[25] He makes a case for this in his 1784 essay "An Answer to the Question: What Is Enlightenment?" (WIE) (8:35–420).

self-discipline of reason, a self-discipline that enables the proper articulation of the limits and the ends of finite human reason. Such self-discipline is needed inasmuch as humanity lives out its moral vocation within the finite conditions of both the determinate natural causality of the material world and the concrete historical workings of society and culture; in the absence of this self-discipline, reason's engagement with the finite conditions of its human exercise is subject to various forms of "transcendental illusion," both theoretical and practical, that deflect it from the trajectory leading to its proper end.

This task is one Kant articulates in a number of texts as the highest good possible in the world, a good that he indicates takes shape in consequence of humanity's participation in the historical accomplishment of the unity of nature and freedom as the final end of humanity's use of reason. Participating in the accomplishment of this good, as this Element argues, constitutes the distinctive moral vocation that reason enjoins upon humanity. This vocation will be shown to consist concretely in humanity's exercise of its moral freedom to bring about the individual and the social conditions that conjointly make historical progress toward making possible the highest good in the world. Chief among the social conditions for historical progress toward such good is constructing a cosmopolitan world political order for establishing an enduring peace among nations, a task for which politics and religion are called upon to play mutually supportive roles. In short, the larger anthropological trajectory of the critical project that aims toward articulating the distinctive place of humanity in the cosmos may be said to have as one of its important concrete outcomes a political one: the legitimation of the project of peace-making on a global scale as a central mark of the moral vocation of humanity in history.[26]

On Kant's account, bringing about an order of lasting peace among peoples through human freedom exercised in mutual respect for one another is thus central to the accomplishment of this human vocation. *In establishing lasting peace, humanity will bring freedom and nature together as a fitting moral accomplishment.* This is an accomplishment that emerges from a human culture that has been reflectively shaped in accord with the exercise of self-governing practical reason. Kant specifically designates this state of international peace as "the highest political good" (MM 6:355) – it is the accomplishment of a definitive order for the external and enforceable regulation of the conduct of

---

[26] This stands in tension with interpretations of Kant's view that place his treatment of war within the "just war tradition." For discussions that place Kant instead on a trajectory aligned, not with justifications of war, but with its elimination, see H. Williams, *Kant and the End of War: A Critique of Just War Theory* (New York: Palgrave Macmillan, 2012) and T. Mertens, "Kant and the Just War Tradition," in *From Just War to Modern Peace Ethics*, ed. H. G. Justenhoven and W. A. Barbieri (Berlin: W. de Gruyter, 2012), pp. 231–247.

nations in relation to one another that bars them from resorting to force of arms as a mode for the settlement of disputes arising among them. While not in itself sufficient for the achievement of the entirety of the highest good for humanity, it does serve as both a social marker for and a necessary element in the enactment of the full and final achievement of that good.

Within the context of Kant's overall articulation of humanity's moral vocation, I think that there is reason to extend Kant's account of the significance of the establishment of an international cosmopolitan order for enduring peace beyond the ambit of the political, the field for external and enforceable regulation of the conduct of nations. Although the establishment of an international order for enduring peace will be a political achievement, it is also an achievement in which the social dynamics of critically disciplined religion have a role to play. I believe that this role can be articulated in terms of Kant's account of the dynamics of the ethical commonwealth, the central social element of his account of critically disciplined religion. These dynamics exhibit the steadfast recognition and respect for the full mutuality of our human freedom that provides a moral horizon for a cosmopolitan world order. They might even be characterized, as is explicated in the last section, as standing as the polar opposite of the image Thomas Hobbes used in his depiction of humanity's "state of nature": a field of constant warfare in which we all are set against one another (*bellum omnium contra omnes*) in endless zero-sum opposition in which there are, always and inevitably, "losers." In contrast, the dynamics of the mutuality of human freedom in the realm of ends that Kant envisions as an ethical commonwealth serve, not as an engine for conflict, but as the enabling conditions for "the true Church," as "the moral people of God," to play a significant role in the historical establishment of peace among the peoples of the world.[27]

The extension I propose arises on the basis of construing the establishment of a cosmopolitan order of lasting peace through the exercise of human freedom to be the external political counterpart of the moral community, the ethical commonwealth, that Kant envisions as the "true church" founded in moral hope. This community emerges from and is empowered by the "moral faith" – i.e., the hope – that humanity can make concretely possible a full social enactment of the mutuality of human freedom in the workings of history; in terms of a long-standing Christian theological image, such full enactment of the mutuality of

---

[27] See Rel. 6:124: "Such therefore is the work of the good principle – unnoticed to human eye yet constantly advancing – in erecting a power and kingdom for itself within the human race, in the form of community according to the laws of virtue that proclaims the victory over evil and under its dominion, assures the world of an eternal peace."

human freedom in history could be considered to instantiate "the kingdom of God on earth."

Construed in these terms, this suggests that the establishment of a cosmopolitan world order for peace, as a moral demand upon humanity, has religious as well as political significance. A world order based upon a mutuality that orders the external relationships among human national communities (and is thus political) into a stable condition of peace would indicate a social empowerment of human moral freedom that, on Kant's account, reaches its complete instantiation religiously as and in the full mutuality of moral recognition empowering agents in the ethical commonwealth. The ethical commonwealth provides the social empowerment that humanity requires in order to overcome the forms of social divisiveness that lie at the root of war. In this way, the ethical commonwealth comports well with another long-standing image, that has its roots in Hebrew scripture, that envisions a "peaceable kingdom" as fundamental feature of the social dynamics that constitute the kingdom of God (Is. 11:1–9; 65:17–25). This social empowerment, which takes form as the ethical commonwealth, thus stands as the polar opposite of Hobbes's "state of nature," in that the encountered difference of the "other" evokes recognition and welcome, rather than erasure and opposition. This empowerment – which Kant sees modeled in religious terms by the life and death of Jesus that "most strikingly displays the contrast between the children of heaven and the bondage of a mere son of earth" (Rel. 6:82) – then makes it possible to consider the efforts of human freedom exercised on behalf of a cosmopolitan world order for peace to be rendered religiously as human participation in the moral work of God.

3 Critique and Cosmopolitanism: The Anthropological Shaping of Religion and Politics

Here I present the second stage of the argument connecting religion and politics in Kant's critical project. It begins with a "snapshot" of Kant's philosophy of religion that focuses on an issue that has long vexed his critics and commentators: What is his attitude and assessment of Christianity? Should Kant be considered a friend or a foe of Christian doctrine and practice? This important question touches upon a number of substantive philosophical and theological issues about evil, sin, freedom, and forgiveness. The purpose in making it the initial focus of this section, however, is not to offer a resolution of these issues; it is, instead, to present a "test case" for the consequences that making a shift to an anthropological perspective upon the critical project has for understanding and interpreting Kant's treatment of religion. For purposes of this test case, moreover, it is useful to note that it is not making the claim that the "friend or foe" question is one that arises solely or even primarily in consequence of reading Kant from an epistemological perspective and/or as the herald of the end of metaphysics; it is a question that will continue to be consequential even when Kant's account is interpreted, as it is here, anthropologically. This test case, instead, points to what often gets overlooked in Kant's account of religion in consequence of too narrow a focus on its application to the specifics of Christianity rather than on his more fundamental concern: identifying the role that religion, as a human phenomenon, plays in the critical project's efforts provides us with an enlarged self-understanding of our human place in the cosmos. What gets overlooked from this narrow focus are the very anthropological elements within his account of religion that help to locate the role this account plays within the larger critical enterprise as well as the features of Kant's treatment of religion that provide important links to his political philosophy.

I then proceed to offer a similar snapshot of Kant's political philosophy, focused on two related issues that have often divided commentators who engage with this part of Kant's work. The main text at issue is Kant's essay from 1795, "Toward Perpetual Peace," in which he offers a proposal outlining the steps that nations of the world should begin to take for putting an end to warfare among themselves. Despite the details his proposal provides, it leaves unsettled the question of the precise form and structure that is to be given to the institutional arrangements needed to establish an order of enduring international peace. Was Kant envisioning the establishment of a single world government that would supplant the sovereignty of individual nations and remove the basis on which they legitimate their right to go to war? Or did he envision, instead, an association of still sovereign nations that would establish enforceable mechanisms to settle issues that previously led nations to resort to force of arms against one another?

Correlative to this issue about the concrete political structure Kant proposes for the achievement of perpetual peace is a second one that bears upon the extent to which he considered it to be even possible as an enduring human accomplishment. Did he envision such an order for peace as a stable and lasting condition that humanity could and would concretely achieve in history or, instead, only as an aspirational ideal for future generations to try, at best, to approximate. More specifically, did Kant take the establishment of a cosmopolitan world order – be it in the form of a "world state" or of a set of supranational bodies to adjudicate disputes between nations on peaceful terms – to be a historically achievable goal for humanity, a goal for which there might be measures or benchmarks for evaluating progress toward its accomplishment? Or was his proposal simply an ideal put forth as a "compass point" to encourage efforts at partial and ad hoc amelioration of the conditions that lead to war, even if they ultimately fail to bring about lasting peace?[28]

As in the case of the snapshot of Kant's philosophy of religion, the goal of the discussion of these elements of Kant's political philosophy is not to resolve these contested issues; it is, instead to use these questions as a test case from which to locate some of the important aspects of Kant's political philosophy that bear upon the fundamental anthropological trajectory of the critical project. These then provide important points of reference for the work of the next stage of the argument (Section 4), which is to identify and articulate the points of connection and convergence that link religion and politics together in the larger anthropological trajectory of Kant's critical enterprise.

3.1 Kant on Religion: A Snapshot

Kant's writings on religion, most prominently his four-part treatise, *Religion within the Boundaries of Mere Reason* (1793), have long been objects of controversy for philosophers and theologians. In stark terms, the question is whether Kant should be considered a friend or an enemy of Christian beliefs and practices. In the course of more than two centuries of Kant commentary and interpretation, a clear-cut consensus on Kant's stance has yet to emerge. In fact, an extensive body of essays and books published on both sides of the Atlantic in the past four decades testifies to the continuing vigor of the contention over Kant's assessment of religion in general and the Christian religion in particular.[29] For some, Kant is a formidable foe of both the orthodox doctrinal

---

[28] See P. Kleingeld, *Kant and Cosmopolitanism: The Philosophical Ideal of World Citizenship* (Cambridge: Cambridge University Press, 2012), especially chapters 1 and 2, pp. 13–71, for an account of the historical and intellectual context in which Kant articulated his views and proposals regarding international order and the sovereignty of nations; chapter 2 discusses the developments in Kant's view on the role of sovereign states in the international order and proposes arguments for the view that Kant could and did "consistently defend the continued existence of a plurality of states" (p. 70).

[29] Among the notable earlier works that reopened questions about the interpretation of Kant's treatment of religion and its role within his larger critical project are A. W. Wood, *Kant's Moral Religion* (Ithaca, NY: Cornell University Press, 1970) and M. Despland, *Kant on History and Religion* (Montreal, McGill-Queen's University Press, 1973); also significant is the treatment of Kant in J. Collins, *The Emergence of Philosophy of Religion* (New Haven, CT: Yale University Press, 1967). A short account of some of the more important contributions to this discussion from both sides of the Atlantic through the mid-1990s can be found in the "Further Reading" list R. M. Adams compiled as part of his "Introduction" to the translation of *Religion within the Boundaries of Mere Reason and Other Writings* for the series Cambridge Texts in the History of Philosophy (Cambridge: Cambridge University Press, 1998), pp. xxxv–xxxvii. The "Editor's Introduction," by C. L. Firestone and S. R. Palmquist, to *Kant and the New Philosophy of Religion* (Bloomington: Indiana University Press, 2006), pp. 1–39, provides an overview of English-language interpretations of Kant's treatment of religion, with special attention to the discussion subsequent to the publication of Wood's and Despland's books. Among the latest

articulations of Christianity and what have historically been its hierarchical forms of organization and governance. He is a major progenitor of modern atheism who cunningly cloaked his aversion to core Christian beliefs in a language of a "moral faith" devoid of any recognizable tenet of the traditional creeds of the Christian church. For others, in contrast, Kant shows at least a circumspect sympathy for certain features of Christian doctrine and its moral practice and might even, on some counts, be considered a religious "seeker." On this view, he is an advocate of a philosophically reformed religion who endeavored to purify the central doctrines of Christianity in ways that would better enable recognition of the "true religion" he sees present as its moral core; this core is constituted by human agents steadfastly enacting the moral call that reason places upon their freedom and responsibility to accord to one another the mutual respect due to them as members of a kingdom of ends. For still others, his accounts of religion "wobble" between, on one hand, offering lines of sharp criticism undercutting the credibility of central Christian doctrines and the value of its ritual practices and, on the other, exhibiting reserved, even resigned acquiescence to the moral distance that human beings have created between the lofty ideal of the true, invisible church as a moral community of equal and mutually responsible moral agents and the deeply flawed instantiations of that ideal provided by the "visible church" up to this point in the course of human history.[30]

Embedded within this contention about Kant's evaluation of the truth of Christian doctrines and of the moral quality of its practices is a more general question about the role that Kant's accounts of religion play within the larger philosophical enterprise he calls critique. Are these accounts simply an articulation of the negative consequences for claims to religious knowledge that ensue from the principles of his critical philosophy and do these cognitive consequences thereby render religion of no value for human life and activity? Or does Kant think that, despite these negative consequences for cognitive claims about God made on behalf of religion, there is still some auxiliary role for religion to play as humanity moves along a trajectory he sees taking it toward moral adulthood? Or, finally, might his writings on religion even delimit the engagement of human finite reason upon religion as a distinctive dimension of human activity, one that has a valuable role in completing the human moral endeavor of critique in a fitting way by bringing human reason itself, as it can be historically

---

contributions to this discussion is a collection of essays, *Kant and the Question of Theology*, ed. C. L. Firestone, N. A. Jacobs, and J. H. Joiner (Cambridge: Cambridge University Press, 2017).

[30] The image of "wobbling" comes from G. E. Michalson Jr., *Fallen Freedom: Kant on Radical Evil and Moral Regeneration* (Cambridge: Cambridge University Press, 1990), pp. 8–10, 125–142.

instantiated in the workings of human community, to its final end in the attainment of the highest good possible in the world?

On the first view, the principles of Kant's critical philosophy place strict limits upon any human effort to cognize or comprehend, be it religiously or philosophically, God as a transcendent "object," inasmuch as such an object cannot in principle be represented in a concept subject to the spatial and temporal forms of human sensible intuition that are requisite conditions for human knowing. These limits thus undercut any claims religion might make to provide us with knowledge of a transcendent God and, concomitantly, with knowledge of an immortal soul as a constitutive element of our humanity. These critical principles allow us, at most, only to "postulate" God as an "Idea," a "regulative" moral ideal that functions to reduce religion to nothing more than a trope for consistent adherence to the fundamental principle of universal morality that Kant calls the "categorical imperative." As a result, critique serves as a vehicle for the secular displacement of religion from its hitherto formative role in Western culture. Critique forestalls the very kind of "transcendental illusion" – a claim to know that which is in principle unknowable for our finite human capacities – for which religion long served as a key locus.[31] On this view, Kant's critical philosophy is among the intellectual forces of modernity standing at the head of the queue that tolls the death knell of God and of religion.[32]

The second view, which allows religion a subordinate role in the critical enterprise, has been advanced in many variations by a wide array of philosophical and theological commentators who take Kant's treatment of religion to be more multifaceted than the relentlessly critical assault portrayed by the first. This second view comports well with an understanding of Kant more as a reformer of and for religion than as one who was, in the pungent phrase of his contemporary Moses Mendelssohn, "the all-destroying" one, bringing to a definitive end the metaphysics for which the transcendence of God had served, at once, as keystone and foundation.[33] Among the versions of this view can be found ones that have been influential in nineteenth- and twentieth-century Christian theology, predominantly but not exclusively among Protestant

---

[31] W. J. Abraham, "Divine Agency and Divine Action in Immanuel Kant, in *Kant and the Question of Theology*, pp. 138–158, offers an intriguing proposal for how theologians concerned to affirm a core set of Christian doctrines might both recognize the theological acumen with which Kant deals with them even while putting aside the "epistemological shovel" with which he sought to bury efforts to render the particularity of divine actions (theoretically) intelligible.

[32] Michalson's later book, *Kant and the Problem of God* (Oxford: Blackwell, 1999), takes the view that Kant's work plays a key role in the emergence of atheism in the nineteenth century.

[33] M. Mendelssohn's epithet for Kant (*des alles zermalmenden Kants*) comes from the preface to *Morgenstunden* (1785), one of the key texts in the "Pantheism Controversy" of 1785–1789 that eventually evoked a response from Kant in the essay "What Does It Mean to Orient Oneself in Thinking?" (1786).

theologians who perceived strong theological resonances both in Kant's deeply rooted "apophaticism" – i.e., a principled refusal to make any positive claims about the attributes of God – and in his focus on the centrality of human moral integrity as the locus for acknowledging God.[34] On this view, though there would be disagreement on whether Kant can properly be called a Christian philosopher – let alone a Christian – there would likely be agreement that his philosophical treatment of religion serves as a useful and a challenging conversation partner upon a range of questions and issues that were and continue to be of theological importance. For many of the commentators engaging Kant in this way, a common concern has often been to locate the extent to which his account may be placed in relation to key coordinates that are constitutive of the major construals of Christian orthodoxy. An unsurprising consequence is that one can find readings of Kant that align him with different – and sometimes quite divergent – theological renderings of Christian doctrines, both Protestant and Catholic.[35]

While these two views diverge in their assessments of the extent to which Kant's critical enterprise regards religion positively or negatively, they do converge in regarding Kant as primarily concerned to engage religion as it has been instantiated in Christian doctrines and practices. Both views do generally recognize that Kant brings into the purview of his arguments some beliefs and practices from traditions other than the monotheisms emergent from the ancient Middle East, but they also take his primary focus to be on the critical assessment of Western Christianity with a view, in the second perspective, to its reform or, especially in the more radically secularizing forms of the first perspective, to its eventual disappearance.[36]

In addition to this agreement that Christianity serves as the main focus of Kant's account of religion, these views tend to converge on another key interpretive marker. Both views are usually framed from a perspective that takes

---

[34] For a discussion of Kant's apophaticism, see P. J. Rossi, "Kant's Apophaticism of Finitude: A Grammar of Hope for Speaking Humanly of God," in *The Linguistic Dimension of Kant's Thought: Historical and Critical Essays*, ed. F. Schalow and R. Velkley (Evanston, IL: Northwestern University Press, 2014), pp. 154–173.

[35] See, for instance, P. J. Rossi, "Reading Kant from a Catholic Horizon: Ethics and the Anthropology of Grace," *Theological Studies* 71, 2010: 79–100. N. Fischer, ed., *Kant und der Katholizismus. Stationen einer wechselhaften Geschichte* (Freiburg: Verlag Herder, 2005) assembles a wide range of essays that reappraise the reception of Kant's work among Catholic philosophers and theologians in the nineteenth and twentieth centuries.

[36] Although Kant does not offer a sustained treatment of religious plurality in *Religion*, he does provide a number of salient remarks on the import of the variety of human religious beliefs and practices in Part III, Division 1, V–VII (Rel. 6:102–124). Of particular import is his remark that "there is only *one* (true) *religion*; but there can be several kinds of *faith*. – We can say, further, that in the various churches divided from one another because of the difference in their kinds of faith, one and the same true religion can nevertheless be met with" (Rel. 6:108–109).

Kant's efforts to secure the certainty of human knowledge as the main engine driving his enterprise of critique. There is little doubt that delimiting the nature and scope of human knowing, for which the work of Descartes became the almost unavoidable point of reference for the philosophical enterprises of modernity, is an important concern for Kant's critical project. He clearly takes note of this issue in the first of his famous three questions: "What can I know? What should I do? What may I hope?" that, toward the conclusion of the *Critique of Pure Reason,* he enunciates as the interrelated foci for the activities of human reason (CPR A804-805/B832-833). When Kant's work is seen from a standpoint that presupposes the conceptual and interpretive priority of the first question, the critical enterprise becomes first and foremost an epistemological one; its success or failure then rests on the capacity of the limits it places on human cognition to refute decisively the gnawing skepticism that impelled the Cartesian turn to take refuge in the conscious individual subject as the impregnable citadel of certainty. In consequence, whatever role that religion might have in the critical enterprise will need to be indexed to and legitimated by its function (if any) with respect to resolving the epistemological concerns that inform and direct it.

In consequence of this dual interpretive convergence, both perspectives, even as they disagree with one another in assessing Kant's friendliness or hostility to religion, nonetheless do agree on what provides the scale with which to judge and calibrate his stance.[37] It is measured in terms of his acceptance, rejection, and/or revision of specific Christian doctrines and practices. In addition, both perspectives generally agree on the interpretive framework – an epistemic limit upon the claims of metaphysics – within which to place (or not to place) religion as a functioning element in the critical enterprise. Religion's (i.e., Christianity's) role, if any, in the critical enterprise is scaled in relation to the measure by which its claims can be cognitively licensed (or disallowed) by principles of critical reason. Kant famously (and cryptically) enunciated this in the preface to the second edition of the *Critique of Pure Reason*: "Thus I have had to deny **knowledge** in order to make room for **faith**" (CPR Bxxx).

As a contrast and counterpoint to these two perspectives for reading and assessing Kant's treatment of religion within his critical philosophy, this Element has been proposing a basis upon which to construct an alternative perspective. The basis for this alternative consists in making at least two shifts that would alter the interpretive convergence operative in the two perspectives on Kant's attitude toward Christianity outlined earlier.

---

[37] Note that this disagreement can also be manifest *within* the second perspective. For some, what makes Kant's program of reform friendly rather than hostile to religion is precisely that it makes conceptually and practically possible a "religion without God."

The first shift would delimit the scope of religion in Kant's account beyond its specific instantiation in Christian belief and practice by taking that account to be engaging with religion as a general human, i.e., anthropological, phenomenon for which Christianity provides one, albeit crucial, instance. A key element in this shift is giving more focused attention to the sociocultural, historical, and political dimensions that enter into Kant's account of religion than has often been the case in the prevailing readings of that account. The significance of these contextual aspects for Kant's account of religion as a human phenomenon may have been too readily overlooked in consequence of too narrow a focus of interpretive attention on Kant's treatment of Christian doctrinal topics, most notably ones such as "justification by faith/grace" that were central in the controversies of the sixteenth-century Protestant Reformation.[38]

The second shift would correlatively enlarge the frame of reference from which to read his critical enterprise beyond that provided by concerns about the scope and certainty of human knowledge. This shift also emerges, at least in part, from a consideration of the social dimension of the critical project, a dimension that becomes more manifest in the writings in which Kant begins to sketch, as his critical project develops, the historical, cultural, and political consequences that ensue from a critically disciplined exercise of human finite reason. Of key import here is the integral role these social dimensions of the critical project play in articulating that project's full scope. They are fundamental to Kant's efforts to articulate a cosmopolitan perspective as the public and social shape of the critically disciplined framework from which to view the moral scope of human action to shape history in accord with the ends of reason – of which the most central is the end made incumbent on humanity by the categorical imperative "there shall be no war."[39] These efforts form a central part of the basis for proposing, in the third stage of this argument, that religion and politics play convergent roles in the articulation and the execution of Kant's critical project.[40] On this account, a critically disciplined religion, reflectively

---

[38] Ironically, this interpretive perspective, which takes Kant to be providing, in the first instance, a critical reformulation of a specific *theological* understanding of "justification" – i.e., one formed in the matrix of Lutheran/Reformed/Pietist influences at work in theologies of the eighteenth-century Prussian Church – has resulted in an overshadowing of the import his treatment of this topic has for a more general *philosophical* account of the significance of religion as a human phenomenon.

[39] MM 6:355: "Now morally practical reason pronounces in us its irresistible veto: *there is to be no war*, neither war between you and me in the state of nature nor war between us as states."

[40] Kant provides a tantalizing suggestion of this in a long footnote at the end of Book 3, division 2 of *Religion* (6:123) in which he proposes a parallel between the challenge that faces human finite reason in the project of constituting an international political order to bring about world peace and the one that faces reason in bringing about "an ecclesiastical unity of faith [that is reconciled] with freedom in matters of faith."

located "within the boundaries of mere reason," serves as the locus for the establishment and functioning of a community of full moral recognition and reciprocity; such a community, as an "ethical commonwealth," provides the moral space that makes possible both a social and an interior acknowledgment of the unconditional force of the imperative "there shall be no war."

The first of the shifts I am proposing for this snapshot reading of Kant's philosophy of religion thus bears upon how broadly or narrowly to construe the scope of religion as it functions in his account. A recalibration of the perspective framed in the two views on Kant's assessment of Christianity outlined earlier might then begin with questions such as: Is Kant's account of religion delimited primarily in relation to a theological map charted in terms of the Christian beliefs, such as sin and redemption, that he explicitly addresses in a text such as *Religion*? In other words, did Kant write this work to place only Christian theology and its auxiliary philosophical speculations "within the bounds of mere reason"? Might Kant's inquiry be, instead, more general in scope, more suitably posed as an inquiry seeking to determine if religion, taken as a larger human phenomenon with significant instantiations beyond specifically Christian forms of belief and practice, has a distinctive role to play in the work of human reason that Kant identifies as critique?[41]

Against the background of this first shift that takes Kant's inquiry into religion to be wider in scope than just examining the cognitive adequacy of Christianity, the second shift I am proposing then arises in the light of the larger issue that Kant's three questions – "What can I know? What should I do? For what may I hope?" (CPR A805/B833) – raise about the fundamental frame of reference from which to read his whole enterprise. In contrast to the long-standing and influential interpretive stance that has been (mostly) presupposed in views focused on Kant's assessment of Christianity, this second interpretive shift takes the main concern of critique to pivot, not primarily upon his first question about knowing, but rather upon his third question, "For what may I hope?" Note that this question is one that Kant expresses more fully a few lines later in this passage by explicitly referring it, not to the first question about knowledge, but to the second question about morality: "If I do what I should, what may I then hope?" (CPR A805/B833). From the standpoint of this question about hope, particularly in this expanded form, the trajectory of the critical enterprise may very well be better aligned along moral coordinates rather than just along the cognitive ones first laid down by Descartes. Even though Kant's

---

[41] J. Collins, *The Emergence of Philosophy of Religion*, characterizes philosophy of religion – for which he sees Hume, Kant, and Hegel as progenitors – as a distinctively modern philosophical enterprise in that it seeks "the properly human significance of religion as it can be grasped and lived cooperatively by all men" (p. viii).

response to the question of hope, as he further elaborates it in this text of this first *Critique*, remains quite schematic, he uses language, noted later in this Element, that suggests that it pivots in a direction that encompasses the moral as well as the epistemic import at stake in that question. That moral import, though not displacing the main focus driving Kant's discussion in this text – to articulate the overall unity and coherence of the enterprise of critique – nonetheless does provide that discussion with a significant moral inflection.[42]

One clear indication of that inflection can be found in the fact Kant articulates "that for which we may hope" in terms of a "moral world." He proposes such a world as one in which "the system of morality is therefore inseparably combined with the system of happiness, though only in the idea of pure reason" (CPR A807/B837). In enabling us to envision such a moral world as the outcome of our human adherence to the moral law – i.e., as the outcome of doing "what I [and all other human rational agents] should do" – hope functions to place humanity's enactment of the unitary workings of critically disciplined human reason into the form of an interconnected social whole constitutive of a moral "world." In this text, Kant portrays such an enactment of the unity of reason abstractly, in terms of what he calls the "interest of human reason" (CPR A805/B832). He conceives such interest as the power driving human reason along the two focal lines of its activity: theoretical inquiry and moral autonomy.[43] In that context, hope functions as the capacity of human reason to envision "the world as it would be if it were in conformity with all moral laws," which he then glosses as envisioning a world "as it can be in accordance with the **freedom** of rational beings and **should** be in accordance with the necessary laws of **morality**" (CPR A808/B836).

Despite the abstractness of Kant's expressions here, it is not difficult to parse the moral inflections they contain; they clearly presage the accounts that the *Groundwork* and the second *Critique* will later provide of human moral freedom as the exercise of practical reason as it governs itself autonomously in

---

[42] Among the remarks Kant makes in CPR that indicate such moral inflection is one from the First Section of "The Canon of Pure Reason," "On the Ultimate End of the Pure Use of Our Reason," regarding the three "transcendental" problems of freedom, God, and immortality: "These [problems] have in turn their more remote aim, namely **what is to be done** if the will is free, if there is a God, and if there is a future world. Now since these concern our conduct in relation to the highest end, the ultimate aim of nature which provides for us wisely in the disposition of reason is properly directed only to what is moral" (A800-801/B828-829).

[43] This discussion of the "interest of reason" in "The Canon of Pure Reason" should be read in the light of Kant's earlier discussion in the Third Section of the Antinomy of Pure Reason, "On interest of Pure Reason in these Conflicts" (CPR A462/B490-A476/B504). S. Neiman, while not directly referencing Kant's terminology of "interest," offers a helpful suggestion about how to construe its "power" as one that drives human reason: it is *a drive to seek intelligibility* – both theoretical and moral – for which the principle of "sufficient reason" stands as a fundamental expression (see *Evil in Modern Thought*, pp. 314–328).

accord with universally binding moral law. It is of no little significance, more-over, that in the second *Critique*, Kant further elucidates the relationship between the interests that drive theoretical and practical uses of human reason in a way that assigns primacy to reason's practical, i.e., moral interest (CPrR 5:119–121). A number of essays from the 1790s also flesh out the primacy assigned to the practical use of reason in social, political, and historical terms that, first, bear upon the coordinate roles that religion and politics play in critically governed human efforts to attain the ends of reason and, second, suggest the enactment of a cosmopolitan world order for peace as a significant locus upon which their roles converge.[44]

The presence of a moral "inflection" in the schematic account that the first *Critique* gives of hope and its function in construing the systemic unity of the critical project does not, however, directly indicate how an interpretive pivoting of Kant's account of religion in the direction of the question of hope might bear upon the place of religion in the critical project. In the course of his later writings, Kant offers a few pointers that are more direct when he recurs to the issues he schematically treats here by engaging them as questions about how the project of critique enables us better to construe the end(s) of reason. These are significant questions inasmuch as Kant takes those ends to bear upon what he sees as the moral vocation and destiny of the human species. While portions of *Religion*, as well as a number of his occasional essays, speak to these questions, a particularly useful place from which to start an examination of how these later texts bear upon the place of religion in the critical project is found in two brief texts in which Kant explicitly returns to the three questions he posed in "The Canon of Pure Reason." In these texts, he again poses the three questions from the first *Critique* as the crucial foci of the critical project – but he now offers two short but significant amplifications to what he wrote in that work.

Here are the texts that provide these amplifications. The first is from a letter to Carl Friedrich Stäudlin, a theologian at Göttingen, dated May 4, 1793. It accompanied a copy of the recently published *Religion within the Boundaries of Mere Reason*.

> The plan I prescribed for myself a long time ago calls for an examination of the field of pure philosophy with a view to solving three problems: (1) What can I know? (metaphysics). (2) What ought I to do? (moral philosophy). (3) What may I hope? (philosophy of religion). A fourth question ought to follow, finally: What is man? (anthropology, a subject on which I have lectured for

---

[44] Among the more significant of these are "On the Common Saying: That May Be Correct in Theory But It Is of No Use in Practice," AA 8:279–309 (1793) and "An Old Question Raised Again: Is the Human Race Constantly Progressing?" Second part of *The Conflict of the Faculties*, 4:80–95 (1798).

over twenty years). With the enclosed work, *Religion within the Limits [of Reason Alone]*, I have tried to complete the third part of my plan. (Corr. 11:429)

The second is from the *Jäsche Logic*, a teaching manual published in 1800 in Kant's name, by one of his students:

> The field of philosophy in this cosmopolitan sense can be brought down to the following questions:
>
> 1. *What can I know?*
> 2. *What ought I to do?*
> 3. *What may I hope?*
> 4. *What is man?*
>
> *Metaphysics* answers the first question, *morals* the second, *religion* the third, and *anthropology* the fourth. Fundamentally, however, we could reckon all of this as anthropology, because the first three questions relate to the last one. (JL 9:25)

Of significance in these amplifications is that they explicitly orient the import of these questions toward religion and anthropology, directions not articulated in the counterpart text in the first *Critique*. Both amplifications correlate the three questions posed in the first *Critique* to a field of philosophical inquiry – the first question to metaphysics, the second to moral philosophy, and the third to religion.[45] The amplification in the *Jäsche Logic* not only adds the fourth question – "What is humanity?" – correlated to anthropology, it explicitly takes this anthropological question to be the one that links together the first three: "Fundamentally, however, we could reckon all of this as anthropology, because the first three questions relate to the last one."

Brief though Kant's amplifications may be, they point to a key role that, at this later stage of the critical project, he suggests that religion, as a human phenomenon, is called upon to play in that enterprise. It is, in the first instance, no small matter that Kant, in both of these later passages, associates the question of hope with religion and its reflective counterpart, philosophy of religion, and that, in the letter to Stäudlin, he also explicitly refers to *Religion* as the work in which he has addressed the question of hope as "part of his plan." This remark to Stäudlin might also be read as an allusion to a claim Kant makes in the preface to

---

[45] Kant's remarks here also complicate interpretive efforts to articulate the relationship of this triad of questions to the work of the triad of texts that he titled *Critique*. This effort is further complicated by the facts that: a) even though Kant treats aspects of "faith" and the "moral proof" of God in the concluding sections of the third *Critique*, that work does not explicitly or extensively engage religion from the standpoint of his critical enterprise and b) in the later work, *Religion*, that does explicitly and extensively engage religion from a critical standpoint, he did not use "Critique" as its title or explicitly articulate the bearing of this work upon that enterprise.

Religion in which he articulates the question of hope in the following terms: "for it cannot possibly be a matter of indifference to reason how to answer the question *What is then the result of this right conduct of ours?"* (Rel. 6:5). Taken in concert with each other, these remarks offer some support to the view that Kant took an engagement with religion to be an important component of his critical project rather than an ancillary consideration; in view of their brevity, however, they provide only a general direction for this engagement and thus leave unsettled important details of how such engagement specifically contributes to the work and the outcome of the critical enterprise. Neither do they seem clearly to provide pointers indicating an unmistakable connection or convergence upon key dimensions of Kant's writings on politics. To find such pointers, we need to look at Kant's writings on politics to identify elements that articulate its bearing upon his larger critical enterprise, particularly those that indicate how humanity's enactment of its moral vocation serves in the circumstances of human history and culture as the concrete locus for the juncture of nature and freedom.

3.2 Kant on Politics: A Snapshot

Kant's forays into political philosophy, which often intersect with his philosophical readings of human history, society, and culture, have also been subject to a variety of interpretations, some of which stand in strong contrast to one another. In keeping with one important strand of Enlightenment political thought, Kant is a proponent of a "republican" organization of political authority in which there is a separation of legislative, judicial, and executive powers (MM 6:313); he sees the citizens of a republican state as the fundamental source of political authority, even as he supports the full placement of executive power in the hands of a monarch, such as the emperors who were sovereigns in Kant's native Prussia (MM 6:316–318). He also restricts voice and vote in legislative processes to male property holders, whom he considers the only ones qualified to be "active citizens" (MM 6:313–315). Though he expressed considerable sympathy for the aims and ideals of the French Revolution,[46] he unequivocally condemned the execution of King Louis XVI: "It is the formal *execution* of a monarch that strikes horror in a soul filled with the idea of human rights" (MM 6:321). At the basis of the ideas and principles of Kant's political philosophy that remain influential to this day, moreover, is his insistence on the centrality, both for our thinking and for our conduct, of the dignity of the individual human person, a dignity has its basis in the freedom that constitutes us all equally as

---

[46] Notably in "An Old Question Raised Again: Is the Human Race Constantly Progressing?" CF7:85–87.

moral agents. The following passage from the *Groundwork of the Metaphysics of Morals* (1785) sets forth the core elements of his thinking: "Now morality is the condition under which alone a rational being can be an end in itself, since only through this is it possible to be a law-giving member in the kingdom of ends. Hence morality, and humanity insofar as it is capable of morality, is that which alone has dignity" (G 4:435). Kant's emphasis upon the centrality of the dignity of the person and the respect due to each person in accord with that dignity has subsequently played a key role in the elaboration of human rights as a touchstone for much of the political and moral culture of Western modernity.

Each of the particular subjects mentioned earlier has a bearing upon the placement of Kant's political philosophy within the ambit of his critical enterprise; yet a more encompassing subject in Kant's writings on politics has the most import for the task of this Element. This is a subject that has direct bearing upon the identification and articulation, in concrete social terms, of the moral vocation in history to which Kant sees humanity called in virtue of its exercise of reason; this is the vocation to participate, through the exercise of moral freedom, in the historical enactment of the highest good possible in the world. This encompassing subject is war, insofar as it constitutes the conflictual "state of nature" that provides the condition making the "right to war" the most fundamental "right" that sovereign nations possess (MM 6:343–351),[47] and peace, insofar as "establishing universal and lasting peace constitutes not merely a part of the doctrine of right *but rather the entire final end of the doctrine of right within the limits of mere reason [nicht bloß einen Theil, sondern den ganzen Endzweck der Rechtslehre innerhalb den Grenzen der bloßen Vernunft ausmache]*" (emphasis added, MM 6:355). This subject might even be more pointedly framed as the *human moral responsibility in matters of war and peace* that Kant here identifies as central to humanity's moral vocation to enact the highest good possible in the world. That responsibility, which pertains to humanity both individually and as a species, consists in bringing about a definitive end to the social form of radical evil that we call "war" and, in so doing, establishing a lasting order of peace for the peoples of the world.[48]

---

[47] Compare this passage, however, with Kant's remarks in TPP 8:356–357: "The concept of the right of nations as that of the right *to go to war* is, strictly speaking unintelligible (since it is supposed to be a right to determine what is right not by universally valid laws limiting the freedom of each but by unilateral maxims through force); one would have to mean by it that it is quite right if human beings so disposed destroy one another and thus find perpetual peace in the vast grave that covers all the horrors of violence along with their authors."

[48] See P. J. Rossi, "War: The Social Form of Radical Evil," in *Kant und die Berliner Aufklärung: Akten des IX. Internationalen Kant-Kongresses*, Band 4, ed. V. Gerhardt, R.-P. Horstmann, and R. Schumacher (Berlin: W. de Gruyter, 2001), pp. 248–256.

War and humanity's responsibility for bringing it to an effective and perma-
nent end is a matter of central concern in Kant's writings on international
relations; it is a subject for which he articulates in his 1795 essay "Toward
Perpetual Peace" a concrete proposal for the achievement of a cosmopolitan
world order that would enable nations to work together to establish a stable and
enduring condition of international peace as a central element of the highest
good possible in the world. Other texts that bear upon this subject are the third
section of his 1793 essay "On the Common Saying: "That May Be Correct in
Theory, But It Is of No Use in Practice" and the concluding sections of Part I
of *The Metaphysics of Morals* (1797) dealing with "the right of nations" and
"cosmopolitan right" (§§53–62, "Conclusion," MM 6:343–372). In addition,
a number of remarks he makes in *Religion*, as noted in the next section, point
to how this proposal also bears upon the fundamental trajectory of the critical
project. While there is general agreement that the essay "Perpetual Peace"
stands as an important conceptual touchstone for what has become a still
developing system of international cooperation and adjudication under the
aegis of a recognized body of international law, there continue to be controversies over the intent, scope, and workings of Kant's proposal, as well as for its
continuing import for the current forms of international political order. In
addition – and pertinent to the main argument here – relatively little attention
has been paid to important conceptual resonances that Kant's proposal for
a cosmopolitan world order securing perpetual peace has with the account of
the social and historical significance of the ethical commonwealth that he
elaborates in Part III of *Religion*.

One arena of contention centers upon what Kant envisioned as the concrete
organizational and institutional form that such a system for a peaceful world
order would take. Was he envisioning the establishment of a single world
government, one that would put an end to the sovereignty of individual nations,
thereby removing a key basis on which nations legitimate their right to go to
war? Or did he envision, instead, an association of individually sovereign
nations that would cooperatively establish mechanisms for the settlement
of issues that previously had led them to resort to force of arms against one
another?[49] A second area of dispute focuses on the related question of the extent

---

[49] This tension is itself instanced in Kant's own texts; see, for instance, TP (8:310–311), in which
Kant suggests both that "the coercion that reason itself prescribes" will bring nations "even
against their will, to enter into a cosmopolitan constitution [*in eine weltbürgerliche Verfassung*]"
and that "if this condition of universal peace is still more dangerous to freedom from another
quarter by leading to the most fearful despotism ... this need must still constrain states to enter
into a condition that is not a cosmopolitan commonwealth under a single head [*kein
weltbürgerliches gemeines Wesen unter einem Oberhaupt*], but is still a rightful condition of
federation [*ein rechtlicher Zustand der Föderation*] in accordance with a commonly agreed upon

to which Kant saw his proposal, elaborated in the essay as two sets of "Articles," one "preliminary" and the other "definitive," for a treaty among the nations, as presenting a goal that human beings would be able concretely to achieve at a definitive, foreseeable point in human history.[50] Did he expect these articles to serve as a concrete blueprint for the establishment of an international order for peace within a few generations? Or are they just aspirational, an elaboration of an ideal along which to align policies to reduce possibilities for armed international conflicts, but without any strong expectation that this would result in the total and lasting elimination of war as a potential instrument for the advancement of national policy and interests?

As in the instance of the test case for Kant's philosophy of religion put forth earlier, regarding his stance toward Christianity, the primary reason for noting these controversies over aspects of Kant's proposal for the establishment of an order of world peace is not to make yet another attempt to resolve them. These controversies undoubtedly pose significant questions that bear upon the overall contours and coherence of Kant's account of the political order; the reason for considering them at this point in the argument of this Element, however, is to note their bearing upon and amplification of a set of key markers on which Kant's philosophy of religion, political philosophy, and (arguably) his philosophy of history and philosophy of culture all converge. Three of these markers have already been identified as important for tracking the anthropological trajectory of the critical project: the highest good possible in the world, the final end of reason, and the moral vocation of humanity, as the locus for human reason's enactment of the juncture of nature and freedom.

In this context, attention to the controversies about how Kant envisioned the concrete instantiation of an order of peace for the nations of the world now helps to identify two further markers along that trajectory: a cosmopolitan international order and the ethical commonwealth, each of which underscores the deeply embedded social and relational character both of Kant's account of the political order and of his account of religion. These two markers exhibit distinct but related inflections of the moral relationality fundamental to the anthropological trajectory of the critical project, each of which is significant for articulating the function and importance that politics and religion each have for the task of enacting humanity's moral vocation.

---

right of nations." Compare this, however, to TPP 8:354, a slightly later text, in which Kant writes, concerning the "Second Definitive article for Perpetual Peace," that the "federation of free states" that it prescribes would be "a *league of nations*, which, however, need not be a state of nations" [*ein Völkerbund, der aber gleichwohl kein Völkerstaat*].

[50] The six "Preliminary Articles" are formulated in Section I, TPP 8:343–347; the three "Definitive Articles" are formulated in Section II, TPP 8:350–360.

A cosmopolitan world order provides, as the political inflection it gives to human moral relationality, the framework for an overarching outer, public, and historical instantiation of a relationality of equal respect as persons that we all owe each other as "world citizens." The ethical commonwealth provides, as a religiously modulated inflection on moral relationality, a counterpart framework for an overarching inner, but also mutually recognizable, instantiation of the equal respect as persons we all owe each another in virtue of what Kant terms "a duty *sui generis* not of human beings toward human beings but of the human race toward itself" (Rel. 6:97). Kant specifies this duty as "the promotion of the highest good as a good common to all," which is to be brought about through a union of persons as "a universal republic based on the laws of virtue [*als einer allgemeinen Republik nach Tugendgesetze*]" (Rel. 6:97–98). This universal republic provides a framework of social relationality for the exercise of human freedom that Kant designates as an ethical commonwealth. Of particular significance for the account that Kant sketches for the role of religion in relation both to politics and to the overall critical project is his further articulation (in Book 3 of *Religion*) of the ethical commonwealth as the "invisible" form of human moral community that provides the regulative paradigm of moral relationality toward which the "visible church" should strive to be the complete instantiation.[51]

Distinguishing these two inflections of moral relationality, one political and the other religious, helps to locate Kant's account of the highest good that is specific to the human political order, the establishment of a cosmopolitan order of world peace, with reference to his larger anthropological account of the most encompassing form of the highest good toward which reason directs humanity in its entirety, i.e., the final end of reason constituted by the attainment of the highest good possible in the world. According to the snapshot of Kant's political philosophy presented here, establishing a cosmopolitan order for world peace is not only the highest political good; the order of peace that it brings and maintains may also be considered a concrete instantiation in human history of a requisite condition for the final attainment of the highest good possible in the world. Although a world in which wars have ceased is a necessary condition for the highest good possible in the world, it does not of itself suffice to constitute

---

[51] There is a long-standing issue in the interpretation of Kant that is embedded in efforts to articulate the relationship between the ethical commonwealth as the "relation of human beings to each other inasmuch as they stand jointly under *public juridical laws* (which are all coercive laws)" and "an *ethico-civil* state . . . in which they [human beings] are united under laws without being coerced, i.e. under *laws of virtue* alone" (Rel. 6:95). This is his distinction between "duties of right" (including justice) and "duties of virtue" and the consequent construal of their relationship to each other. For an illuminating recent discussion of this issue, see O. O'Neill, "Enactable and Enforceable: Kant's Criteria for Right and Virtue," *Kant-Studien* 107, 2016, pp. 111–124.

the totality of good in and for the world. From Kant's perspective, it is only a widely encompassing "juridical" – i.e. outward – condition for the attainment of the highest good. Yet even as a juridical condition pertaining to an external social ordering of human conduct in international matters, it is an ordering that is of signal importance in that *what it seeks to extirpate – war – may be considered, in view of its social instantiation of self-preference, the paradigmatic and most challenging social form of radical evil.*[52] In this regard, it is a condition for the attainment of the highest good possible in the world that can be considered to point beyond the concrete political good it instantiates to the framework of the more thoroughgoing moral relationality established in the ethical commonwealth, a mutuality that makes it possible to supersede the obduracy of self-preference.

The highest good possible in the world, in contrast to the highest political good, is not simply a condition that is placed "externally" upon human conduct. It is the final end of reason that *results from* human freedom's enactment of it in the world, and thus enables humanity to fulfill its moral vocation to be the juncture in the world linking nature and freedom. It is a good that is fully and unqualifiedly moral in form, i.e., it is enacted out of the inner human freedom that Kant identifies as the exercise of finite practical reason. Of equal consequence – especially for its relation to the highest political good – is that it is a good that is social both in the form of its enactment and in the conditions for its attainment. This social character is signaled in the social resonances of the array of images, e.g., "moral world," "kingdom of ends," "kingdom of grace," and, most notably, "ethical commonwealth," that Kant uses to designate the form of this good and the context and dynamics that bring it into actuality.

The different inflections Kant gives to these two important characterizations of the highest good – one bearing on the external structuring of an international order for establishing enduring peace, the other bearing on the inner orientation and the dynamics of human relationality, as made socially manifest in an ethical commonwealth – provide the background to complete this snapshot of his political philosophy. They provide a basis from which to articulate Kant's account of the relation between these two characterizations of good, of how this relation bears upon the manner in which humans attain them, and how these are then significant for the complementary roles that religion and politics play in Kant's critical enterprise.

---

[52] One particularly blunt assertion Kant makes about the moral unintelligibility of war is TPP 8:356–357. "The concept of the right of nations as that of the right to go to war is, strictly speaking unintelligible [*läßt sich eigentlich gar nicht denken*]." See P. J. Rossi, "War as Morally Unintelligible: Sovereign Agency and the Limits of Kantian Autonomy," *The Monist* 99:1 (2016): 1–12; doi:10.1093/monist/onv025; "War: The Social Form of Radical Evil."

There is, on one hand, the highest political good, a focal element in his writings on politics and history, that is concretely and historically instantiated as a cosmopolitan international order that will secure lasting peace in human history. There is, on the other hand, the highest good possible in the world, arguably the key focal element for his writings on morality and religion, as well as for the critical project as a whole, that is construed as the "final" and "ultimate" end of human reason. The former good, political in form, emerges in the course of human history, and requires human construction of external, juridical structures that function in the workings of human society. Given that the principles for governing the juridical structure of such a cosmopolitan world order (which Kant formulates as the articles for perpetual peace) pertain to nations in their relations with one another, the agency for the effective working of that structure resides in each nation's sovereign governance as a political entity, i.e., as a state. With regard to its sovereignty, Kant takes the state to be "a moral person [and is] considered as living in relation to another state in the condition of natural freedom and therefore in a condition of constant war" (MM 6:343).

To the extent that such sovereign governance of the political state is taken as modeled on the agency of a moral person, Kant implies, but does not explicitly articulate, that it needs to be shaped by a political/social counterpart to the self-discipline that reason undertakes with respect to individual moral agency in the project of critique, i.e., the formation of a "good will." As the only thing "in the world that could be considered good without limitation" (G 4:393), a good will instantiates the moral relationality that is freely undertaken at the core of human agency; it thus stands as the polar opposite to the Hobbesian agency of obdurate self-preference that forms the "state of nature" and that requires unremitting external coercion to establish and maintain what in the end is merely a semblance of moral relationality.[53] In locating the original context of the state's sovereign agency as a state of nature equivalent to a "condition of war," Kant is harking back to and reprising considerations regarding moral agency in its relation to the social dynamics of human community that he engaged in the opening pages of Part III of *Religion* (Rel. 6:93–102). In that discussion, he explored the interrelated dynamics by which it becomes possible for human moral agents to undertake their exit from the "juridical" state of nature, which they do by the formation of political communities (states), and from the "ethical" state of nature, which they do by the formation of the moral community of full relationality he calls the "ethical commonwealth" and

---

[53] See P. J. Rossi, "War as Morally Unintelligible: Sovereign Agency and the Limits of Kantian Autonomy."

identifies with the "true church." These dynamics form the matrix within which it becomes possible to identify and articulate the relationship between the attainment of the highest political good and the attainment, as the final end of reason, of the highest good possible in the world. As is indicated later in this Element and then elaborated in the final section, the social character of these dynamics, particularly as it takes form as the hope that is characteristic of Kantian "moral faith," is central to this relationship. It thus provides the most fundamental basis from which to construe the complementarity between Kant's political philosophy and his philosophy of religion.

In contrast to the juridical character of the good of the political order, which is one that requires coercion for the establishment of external moral relationality, the good that constitutes the final and ultimate end of human reason emerges in and from humanity's uncoerced and incoercible exercise of freedom. In contrast to – but not thereby in opposition to – the external juridical ordering of the political, Kant conceives such a good as functioning in terms of a freely undertaken, inner moral orientation of relationality that governs the exercise of reason by each and every individual human moral agent.[54] This latter good takes a form that, inasmuch as it issues from the uncoerced exercise of human freedom as it is ordered to relationality, is fully and unqualifiedly moral. This inner ordering to relationality is one that functions in reference to "the moral world" that hope both enables and (morally) requires us to envision as the totality of the good enacted by moral freedom as it is exercised by each and every human agent. In Kant's terminology, the orientation provided by the tropes such as "moral world" or a "kingdom of ends" functions as a "regulative" principle – it enables us to envision the world as it ought to be as a project for our moral freedom to enact.[55]

In placing the establishment of an order of lasting peace among peoples as a condition for attaining the highest good possible in the world, Kant is indicating that this concrete social and historical achievement, brought about as

---

[54] This inner governance encompasses *the exercise of moral reason by agents who hold sovereign political power that they are entitled to exercise coercively in virtue of their standing in the juridical order.* See the distinction Kant makes between the "political moralist" and the "moral politician" in Appendix I of TPP (8:371–380). This discussion suggests that, in Kant's own context, the categorical imperative "there shall be no war" is in the first and most important instance, *incumbent upon the sitting monarchs of the various nations of Europe.* If this is correct, "Perpetual Peace" could very well be properly read as a call for their moral conversion: they are the agents who, in virtue of their sovereign power, can make it possible for nations to leave the international "state of nature," and thereby to overcome the social form of obdurate self-preference that is the "radical evil" of war.

[55] S. Neiman understands Kant's view of a regulative principle to be "not an idea we derive from the world but one we bring to it [it is] a drive essential to reason itself" (*Evil in Modern Thought*, p. 320; see *The Unity of Reason*, pp. 89–94).

the work of human freedom exercised in mutual respect for one another, stands as central element for accomplishing humanity's moral vocation to serve as the juncture of nature and freedom. In establishing lasting peace, humanity will bring freedom and nature together in a way that will stand as a fitting *moral* accomplishment, one that emerges from a human culture that has been reflectively shaped in the course of its history in accord with the exercise of self-governing practical reason. The establishment of a definitive order for the external and enforceable regulation of the conduct of nations in relation to one another will bar them from resorting to force of arms as a mode for the settlement of disputes arising among them. It will, in effect, close the curtain of history upon the "state of nature" that Hobbes envisioned as ceaseless warfare that, at best, could only be curbed by the relentless coercion of the all-encompassing Leviathan-like sovereignty of the state. While the establishment of a cosmopolitan world order would not in itself be sufficient for the achievement of the entirety of the highest good for humanity, it does serve, on Kant's account, as a necessary element on the way to the full and final achievement of the highest good he envisions as the task that is set for humanity's moral vocation.

In consequence, some elements of the relationship between these two forms or modalities of the highest good can be clearly articulated. The most obvious is that the highest political good of establishing an international order that secures world peace, even though it clearly is a good "in the world," does not in Kant's view constitute by itself the entirety of the highest good in the world. The highest political good can be understood, nonetheless, as concretely constituting at least one part of that highest good that humanity is called upon to make possible in the world through the exercise of freedom. It can also be plausibly argued that Kant also takes it to be one of the most fundamental conditions requisite for the attainment of that latter, fully completed form of the highest good; the absence of an enduring order of world peace would count tellingly against whatever other state of good in the world in which humanity may enact being the achievement of "the highest good in the world."

In these instances, the relationship in question bears upon the highest political good as an element in and/or as a condition for the achievement of a more encompassing condition of good – the final or ultimate good for humanity. The directionality of the relation in both instances goes from the less encompassing good (in this case, the political) to a fully encompassing good that is understood as final and ultimate for humanity as a whole and in all its aspects. In consequence, some of the difficulties that arise in specifying further dimensions of their relationships arise from the abstractness with which Kant characterizes what constitutes the highest good possible in the world in contrast to the concreteness with which he is able to specify the elements and shape of the highest political good. In the case of the highest political good, he concretely spells out important elements as six preliminary and three definitive articles for a world order of perpetual peace – e.g., "Standing armies shall in time be abolished altogether"; "The civil constitution in every state shall be republican" (TPP 8:345, 349). In contrast, he construes the moral world that provides for the possibility for the attainment of the highest good in quite abstract terms, e.g. the ones he uses in the first *Critique*: It is "the world as it would be if it were in conformity with all moral laws" (CPR A808/B836).

Despite the abstract generalities in Kant's characterization of the moral world in which humanity is called upon to enact the highest good possible in the world, there are elements in the account that *Religion* provides of the ethical commonwealth that point to concrete features of the moral relationality it provides for humanity's enactment of its moral vocation. In that account, the ethical commonwealth constitutes more than just a contingent gathering or temporary union of moral agents who are consistent in their intent to respect the moral law that reason enjoins as a categorical imperative. It is, rather, a set of mutually recognized and intentionally framed *social conditions and practices* for enabling conduct and practices that lead to the enactment of the highest good possible in the world. These conditions can plausibly be rendered as concrete amplifications and institutionalizations of the condition of social relationality among free, finite moral agents that Kant had previously termed a "kingdom of ends."[56] This social condition is one that provides for the possibility of full and enduring instantiations of the dynamic of mutual moral recognition that stands as a constitutive feature of human finite freedom.

It is a condition, moreover, in which the highest good *pertains to humanity as a whole*, i.e., as the object of a distinctively social hope and demand orienting the exercise of human freedom. As the next section indicates, it is this social form of the highest good that is fittingly evoked not just by tropes with ethical and political resonances, such as a moral world, the kingdom of ends, and an ethical commonwealth, but also by images that have theological and religious ones: a "kingdom of grace" and "the kingdom of God." In suggesting a complementarity among these tropes, Kant may very well also be suggesting that religion, in the purified mode he terms moral faith, does not serve simply as an optional addendum to the critical enterprise but rather provides a crucial pointer to the social form that is requisite to mark the completion of the work of reason in and for human history: the highest good possible in the world, the

---

[56] Education, freedom of public discourse and the press, and the "visible church" are three of the important spheres for instantiation and institutionalization of the dynamic of mutual moral recognition.

final and ultimate end of human reason that marks the completion of humanity's moral vocation, is attained and enacted in a social form.

4 The Ethical Commonwealth: Social Imperative for Cosmopolitan Peace-Making

This Element initially provided, in Sections 1 and 2, an overview of Kant's critical philosophy as an anthropological enterprise that seeks to articulate the character and the significance of the moral vocation of humanity. That vocation arises from what Kant envisions as the unique status our species holds in the cosmos: humanity is called upon to serve as the juncture that links the causal workings of the natural world (of which humanity is a part) with the moral freedom that is fundamental to the structure and working of human personal agency and is thereby requisite for the operation and flourishing of human life in society and history. Our human engagement with the causal workings of nature and with the personal agency that we exercise in freedom are each under the governance of reason, the deeply rooted drive we have to make sense of the world. Our engagement with the causal workings of nature provides the field for the exercise of our reason as theoretical, in which we seek to explain "how the world works" and to do so in the most comprehensive terms. Our engagement with the world as a locus for human choice and action provides the field for the exercise of our reason as practical, for which we require reason's judgments for discriminating between good and evil and right and wrong as norms for our agency's determination of what to do and how to act. As is the case with the theoretical exercise of reason, practical reason seeks to make sense of the world, but does so in *moral* terms, terms that are referenced to good and evil and right and wrong; in seeking to make moral sense of the world, reason in its practical exercise also does so in the most comprehensive way, i.e., with respect to what Kant terms the highest good possible in the world and to our agency's role in bringing about that good.

Both the theoretical and the practical uses of reason play a role in humanity's efforts to fulfill its moral vocation, but in order for them to do so, they each need to be exercised in accord with a recognition of the limits that our finitude places upon the scope and the capacity of our reason in each of its uses.[57] This recognition of the limits of our human finitude is the outcome of the reflective

---

[57] S. Neiman's observation is pertinent here: "Of the many distinctions Kant took wisdom and sanity to depend on drawing, none was deeper than the difference between God and all the rest of us. Kant reminds us as often as possible of all that God can do and we cannot. Nobody in the history of philosophy was aware of the number of ways we can forget it ... Kant's relentless determination to trace the ways we forget our finitude was matched only by his awareness that such forgetting is natural" (*Evil in Modern Thought*, p. 75).

enterprise Kant calls critique, a project that he considers of vital importance for the proper accomplishment of humanity's moral vocation to serve as the juncture of nature and freedom. In the absence of critique – the reflective recognition and acknowledgment of the limits that our finitude places upon the efforts of reason to make sense of the world (including our human place in that world as morally free agents) – our reason is subject to debilitating illusions. Among these illusions, the most debilitating, in Kant's judgment, are those that, based on misunderstandings of the workings of our freedom in relation to the causal workings of the natural world, lead us to abandon as pointless or illusory our human efforts, be they individual or collective, to be good and to do good in the world and for the world. In the context of these temptations to despair of the value and the effectiveness of our moral efforts, the intellectual and moral discipline that Kant calls a critical metaphysics provides, in contrast, a basis for moral hope in the effectiveness of human action for the accomplishment of good: human beings can, in fact, be effective agents, both individually and in concert with one another, through the proper use of human reason in the concrete contexts of human society and history, in participating in the enactment of the highest good possible in the world. Kant takes the question of hope to be one that we necessarily pose out of a concern for the efficacy of the moral action that reason, in its practical use, enjoins us to do: "for it cannot possibly be a matter of indifference to reason how to answer the question, *What then is the result of this right conduct of ours?*" (Rel. 6:5). The question of hope for the efficacy of our moral conduct for the enacting of good thus provides a fundamental point of reference for the anthropological shape of Kant's critical project. It is a point of reference that, as later discussion of the ethical commonwealth indicates, is drawn from the social character of our finite human moral agency and that bears crucially upon the role critically disciplined reason plays in orienting human political and religious activity to the enactment of good.

The anthropological reading presented here, with its focus on moral hope in the efficacy of human action, is offered as an alternative to what Section 1 termed the standard account of Kant's philosophy, one primarily focused on questions of the possibility of genuine knowledge (epistemology) and of the fundamental character and order of the world (metaphysics) – with the greater weight most often given to epistemology. One consideration on behalf of exploring a different line of interpretation is that, given its strong epistemological focus, the standard account often neglects to provide an adequate and comprehensive basis from which to include other important elements in Kant's work, such as his political philosophy, moral philosophy, philosophy of history and culture, and philosophy of religion, as an integral part of his critical enterprise. This is not an insubstantial consideration, in that there is evidence in Kant's texts indicating that he took these elements to have an integral and important place within his larger project.[58]

So, in place of an epistemological focus that has, on more than one reading, become more narrowly construed than can be well supported from Kant's texts, the anthropological one proposed here takes the following as the main concern driving Kant's philosophical enterprise: what is the place, the role, the significance of humanity, and of what humanity does, within the larger cosmos of which we find ourselves a part? Framing Kant's enterprise in terms of this question, which occupied most of Section 1, provided a basis from which we were offered, in Section 3, snapshots of his philosophy of religion and of his political philosophy to probe the extent to which this anthropological framework provides adequate and appropriate conceptual space for including them as integral to his critical project. Those snapshots offered reasons to think that both religion and politics (as well as their reflective philosophical counterparts) are integral and important for the anthropological work of Kant's critical project to articulate the moral vocation of humanity and to enable humanity to participate as effective agents, individually and socially, in the enactment of the highest good.

This final section builds upon the case, illustrated in those snapshots, that Kant's treatments of politics and religion are integral to his larger critical project, particularly in terms of its focus on the human role in enacting the highest good. From that starting point, this section explores the possibility that not only are those two accounts each integral to the critical project but that they also are complementary to one another. Their complementarity consists in the mutually supportive function they each have in identifying, articulating, and bringing into relation the concrete social character of those aspects of the final end of reason – the political and the religious – that fall within the respective provinces of their activity and reflective articulation as elements of critique as an anthropological enterprise. A central element offered in support of their complementarity is a proposal to extend the significance of the establishment of an international cosmopolitan order for enduring peace that Kant offers in "Perpetual Peace" beyond the ambit of the specific and widely encompassing political sphere of international relations to which it is directed as a plan for an

---

[58] As noted earlier (note 8), Kant's 1784 essay "Idea for a Universal History with a Cosmopolitan Aim" offers a programmatic outline of the bearing that critique, as a key aspect of the development of human reason, has upon the role that culture and society play in the attainment of the moral end set before humanity. Another key discussion with respect to the role of a critically disciplined religion in attaining that moral end can be found in Kant's treatment of the historical establishment of "the kingdom of God on earth" in Part III of *Religion*, most notably 6:115–137.

external and enforceable structure for regulating the conduct of nations. This extension is posed by relating the dynamics of cosmopolitanism to those of the ethical commonwealth, the central social element of Kant's account of critically disciplined religion. These social dynamics are presented as the locus within which the true Church, as the moral people of God, is called upon to play a role in the historical establishment of peace among the peoples of the world that is distinct from, but complementary to and supportive of, that played by a cosmopolitan political order.

The proposal for this extension thus argues that the establishment of the political structures for a cosmopolitan world order for peace may also be construed religiously in reference to the social dynamics of the ethical commonwealth as a key locus for overcoming forces of human divisiveness, particularly as it forms the dynamics of the conflict fundamental to the "state of nature" as a Hobbesian *bellum omnium contra omnes*. In this construal, the establishment of that external political order can be rendered religiously as *a social empowerment of the moral freedom that is requisite in order for humanity to overcome the forms of social divisiveness that lie at the root of war.* This empowerment – which Kant sees modeled in religious terms by the life and death of Jesus that "most strikingly displays the contrast between the children of heaven and the bondage of a mere son of earth" (Rel. 6:82) – makes it possible to consider the efforts of human freedom exercised on behalf of a cosmopolitan world order for peace not only to be directed to establishing new political structures for international order, but also to be the instantiation and enactment of human social participation in the peace-making that constitutes "the moral work of God." Religion, on this account, has a distinctive role in human efforts to secure the order of peace as the highest political good; this role is to constitute a social space of human interaction that, purified of the self-preferential divisiveness constitutive of the "ethical state of nature," empowers the enactment of the full moral mutuality that is requisite for enacting an enduring condition of peace.

This social space is constituted on the basis of what Kant proposes as arguably the most authentic form of human religious practice, i.e., the social dynamics of the ethical commonwealth. This practice originates from the enactment of the full mutual moral recognition constitutive of the social dynamic of the ethical commonwealth. That dynamic takes form as a socially oriented hope that enables us to envision the efficacy of the human enactment of good from the perspective of a moral faith focused beyond the outcome that the exercise of moral freedom has for an individual moral agent. The dynamic of social hope provides a larger horizon from which to view the efficacy of moral freedom, a horizon opening space for a human community to be empowered to live in full mutual moral recognition. In the ethical commonwealth, moral faith expands into a social hope that provides a *social empowerment* of its members to work in concert for the enactment of good in its fully social instantiations, of which a central one will be the establishment, in the political sphere, of an international order of enduring peace. Put in traditional Christian vocabulary, this horizon reorients the way "salvation" is understood and imagined beyond exclusively individual terms – "saving one's soul" – to a more encompassing social horizon in which *each one's salvation is implicated in the salvation of all*: one is (truly and fully) "saved" only if/when *all* are "saved."

Religion, in the guise of such critically disciplined "moral faith," thus not only enables human agents to hope in the moral efficacy of individual enactments of good; it also prepares human agents to envision themselves as members of an ethical commonwealth who are mutually responsible to one another and thereby are empowered to exercise their freedom *as thoroughly and constitutively social*. As mutually responsible members of the ethical commonwealth, human agents are called upon to exercise freedom not simply as it bears upon the hope they may have in regard to their own individual moral destiny (e.g., as hope for personal immortality) but *also – and perhaps more fundamentally – as it bears upon the social outcomes of history and culture that bear upon the destiny of humanity as a whole*. Included as a central element in these social outcomes is the cosmopolitan order of peace that Kant's political philosophy envisions as the good toward which reason, in its juridical guise, points as an appropriate end and, indeed, as the highest political good.

To the extent that Kant's account both of a cosmopolitan world order, which is central to his political philosophy, and of the ethical commonwealth, which is central to his philosophy of religion, arises from his understanding of human freedom as thoroughly and constitutively social, it suggests a deeper and more fundamental line of connection and complementarity between these two elements of his critical philosophy. There are indications of such a connection in his shorter writings on political history from the 1780s and 1790 as well as in his larger treatises from the 1790s, *Religion within the Boundaries of Mere Reason* and *The Metaphysics of Morals*. In these writings, an account of moral hope in the efficacy of human action for the attainment of good informs his discussions of a cosmopolitan perspective and its function in humanity's role in shaping the trajectory of history. Kant articulates cosmopolitanism as a perspective, made possible by the practical interest of reason, from which human agents are enabled to render their activity morally intelligible, not just in terms of its role in making them individually worthy of happiness but also as that activity is an ingredient in the sociocultural matrix that constitutes the

dynamics of history. From this outlook, human agents can construe the workings of their freedom as efficacious not merely with respect to their individual
moral worthiness but also for a socially effective shaping of the historical
trajectory of human society and culture as it is oriented to the enactment of
the highest good possible in the world.

Cosmopolitanism may thus be construed as *a social form of hope for the
enactment of the highest good* that Kant sees as having its origin in the practical
use of reason. It enables us to envision that good *as a social enactment* of human
freedom. On Kant's account of the moral efficacy of human agency, only that
good in which human freedom has a role in effecting can be properly considered
a candidate for being the highest good for our humanity. Hope in its cosmopolitan, i.e., social, form provides human agents a way to envision the exercise
of their freedom not simply as it bears upon their own individual moral
destiny but also as it bears upon the social outcomes of human history and
culture. It envisions the highest good attained through human freedom to pertain
to humanity as a socially and historically situated species with a distinct and
socially inflected moral vocation, not merely to each human agent as a separate
individual.

In addition, this perspective envisions the exercise of human freedom, both
individually and in concert with one another, as itself functioning to shape the
social conditions in which human agency is exercised for attaining this good.
The highest human social good is achieved not through a mere aggregation of
individual efforts, coordinated by a moral analogue to preestablished harmony;
it is achieved through each and every agent's attention to the dynamics of the
mutual respect due one another's freedom in the interactions that shape the
social conditions for dwelling with one another within the finite confines of our
planet. In consequence, the role of a critically disciplined religion here can thus
be framed by reference to the bearing that the dynamic of moral interaction
marking an ethical commonwealth has upon aspects of the social character of
cosmopolitan hope.

For instance, religion, in the form of the social dynamic of mutual respect
enacted by members of the ethical commonwealth, sharpens attention to the
responsibility we bear to and for one another in shaping *all* the social conditions
for our mutual interaction in freedom, such as the external and structural
political conditions of the kind Kant details in the preliminary and definitive
"Articles for Perpetual Peace." Religion, on Kant's account in the third part of
Religion, also moves, under the guidance of reason in history, on a trajectory
from division to unity; he sees the multiplicity of particular ecclesiastical faiths
slowly converging upon a critically disciplined religion that points toward
a future in which the inner unity and universality that is an essential mark of

"the one true religion" can become more publicly manifest (Rel. 6:121–124).[59] On these matters, the full historical establishment of the ethical commonwealth, particularly with respect to the challenges of forming a manifest social unity that brings into cooperation and harmony communities of concretely different "historical faiths," has important parallels to the establishment of an international order for securing lasting peace. This suggests that the forms of inter-religious encounter, dialogue, and cooperation that have arisen in the past century – even as conflicts over religion still fester, at times quite violently – can be viewed from a cosmopolitan perspective as functioning as an important propaedeutic for the project of establishing an international order for enduring peace.[60]

The ethical commonwealth, as the context in which moral faith is empowered as *a constitutively social hope*, thus allows agents to envision this highest political good to be attained through their human freedom to pertain to their humanity precisely as socially and historically constituted as a species, not merely to each agent as an individual.[61] This suggests a way in which the attainment of a cosmopolitan order of enduring peace as the highest political good for humanity can be appropriately rendered religiously: it stands as *the definitive social empowerment* of human freedom, an empowerment that, *by*

---

[59] The two footnotes at Rel. 6:123 indicate Kant's clear perception of the depth of the challenges that need to be faced in both the political and the religious projects for effecting social unity among morally free human agents; not surprisingly, Kant also suggests that overcoming the obduracy of human self-preference is fundamental to meeting these challenges successfully: "There seems to be a propensity in human nature (perhaps put there on purpose) that makes each and every state strive, when things go its way, to subjugate all others to itself, and achieve a universal monarchy but, whenever it has reached a certain size, to split up from within into smaller states."

[60] This connection is made in the mission statement of one of the major organizational platforms for the promotion of interreligious harmony and understanding, the Parliament of the World's Religions: "The Parliament of the World's Religions was created to cultivate harmony among the world's religious and spiritual communities and foster their engagement with the world and its guiding institutions in order to achieve a just, peaceful and sustainable world" (https://parliamentofreligions.org/about/mission; accessed December 28, 2018).

[61] This point bears upon an unresolved issue that, though important for the internal workings of Kant's political philosophy, does not directly bear upon the relationship between his political philosophy and his philosophy of religion under discussion here. The question at stake in this unresolved issue is: what *specific human agents* have the responsibility to bring about the changes in the international political order, such as the abolition of standing armies, requisite for bringing about the conditions for perpetual peace? At first, it seems that Kant, in keeping with his view that political sovereignty is properly invested in the person of a single ruler, i.e., a monarch, would initially place that agency in the hands of each of the sitting monarchs of Europe. Matters get a bit more complicated, however, once the possibility is opened – as Kant seems to do in at least a few places in his texts – that citizens may also have an agential role in this process. For instance, in a republican constitution that provides for citizens to have a say in the use of taxation, these citizens might effectively oppose use of that revenue in support of a standing army as wasteful. See P. J. Rossi, "War as Morally Unintelligible: Sovereign Agency and the Limits of Kantian Autonomy," pp. 1–12.

overcoming the social divisiveness that lies at the root of war, gives the lie to the Hobbesian depiction of "the state of nature" as *bellum omnium contra omnes*. To the extent that both the ethical commonwealth and a cosmopolitan world order envision the definitive social empowerment of human freedom for establishing an order of full human mutuality, they thereby *disempower the social divisions and contentions at the root of war*, the paradigmatic social form of radical evil. They jointly provide conditions for an enduring historical enactment of the social good that moral freedom makes possible by the mutual respect constitutive of the social dynamics of the ethical commonwealth.

The roles of the ethical commonwealth and of a cosmopolitan world order in empowering moral hope thus bear not just on individual moral empowerment and accountability. They also have a fundamental bearing upon humanity's larger moral vocation as a species to serve as the unique juncture between freedom and nature in the workings of the cosmos; they empower a *social hope* in humanity's effective participation together in the enactment of the highest good possible in the world. Kant's comments on the French Revolution in the second part of the *Conflict of the Faculties* (CF 7:85–87) characterize it as an event of social hope: it evokes from its onlookers a recognition of "a moral character of humanity" from which it will be possible to enact moral progress eventuating in the deterrence of war.[62] This social characterization of hope also bears significantly upon the relationship between Kant's political philosophy and his philosophy of religion as it is instanced in Kant's depiction of Jesus as "son of God" (his preferred expression in *Religion*). Within the context of humanity's "species vocation," Kant takes the work of the "son of God" to be such that it opens the possibility for humans to act in a distinctively "godly" manner *in their social interaction with one another*. This godly manner consists of acting in ways that, by resisting and curtailing the radical evil of the divisiveness that leads to conflict, help to bring about the conditions for peace among peoples. Kant suggests this possibility by viewing Jesus as modeling for humanity a redemption from the grip of a radical evil that, *by its corruption of individual moral agency by maxims of self-preference, has led to a pervasive state of social divisiveness*, pointedly imaged by Hobbes as a constant state of war. On Kant's account, this liberation from the bondage of evil, paradigmatically modeled for us in Jesus, thus not only serves to empower fully the moral freedom of individual human agents but also enables the freedom of humanity *as a species* to function effectively in concert toward the attainment of the peace that is an

---

[62] For a provocative discussion of Kant's stance toward the French Revolution and its bearing upon the project of securing perpetual peace, see H. Arendt, *Lectures on Kant's Political Philosophy* (Chicago: University of Chicago Press, 1982), pp. 40–58.

essential component of humanity's participation in the establishment of the highest good possible in the world.

In consequence, Jesus's most godly activity – and, by extension, the most godly activity he models for human beings – was to make it possible for human beings to have the moral freedom to establish and live together in a social order in which they *together* overcome the evil of the social divisiveness leading to war; they do so by manifesting full respect for one another's freedom in the dynamics of an ethical commonwealth that enacts the effective overcoming of such divisiveness.[63] On Kant's account, the most socially significant way in which the Son of God exhibits this godly mode of action is by his establishment of "the Kingdom of God." Kant explicitly characterizes this establishment in terms of an empowerment of human freedom that has social as well as individual effects:

> [B]y exemplifying this principle (in the moral idea) that [a] human being [i.e., Jesus] opened the doors of freedom to all who, like him, choose to die to everything that holds them fettered to earthly life to the detriment of morality; and among these he gathers unto himself "a people for his possession, zealous of good works" under his dominion, while he abandons to their fate all who prefer moral servitude. (Rel. 6:82)

It is also of significance that this passage, indicating this social dimension to Jesus's exemplification of the godly activity of effecting human freedom from bondage to radical evil, is found near the conclusion of Part II of *Religion*, prior to Kant's extensive treatment, in Part III, of the establishment of the ethical commonwealth. In this text from Part II, his arguments, while still primarily focused on the grip that radical evil has upon the dynamics of individual moral agency, are nonetheless strikingly cast in social and political images. His reconstruction of Christian teaching about how God effects human redemption in the person of the Son of God articulates it with an explicit political inflection: redemption is accomplished in the context of a conflict between radical evil and the good principle that Kant frames in terms of *sovereignty*: which of these has a *rightful claim to moral dominion over human beings*? It is a conflict, moreover, in which Kant describes the part that Jesus plays in terms of a revolutionary resistance that puts in peril the sovereignty of "the prince of this world" (Rel. 6:78–84).[64] These political resonances reinforce the function

---

[63] H. Williams, *Kant's Political Philosophy* (Oxford: Basil Blackwell, 1983), p. 268, observes: "The highest political good and the highest moral good can, he [Kant] thinks, only be achieved simultaneously. Nature and individuals will only live in harmony together in a world society when that world society is a world community."

[64] This passage also has some distant echoes, in its portrayal of resistance to the tyranny and whim of a sovereign, to the important passage in the *Critique of Practical Reason* that exhibits, in the

of this passage as a prelude to Part III's more explicit and extensive discussion of the social dimensions of radical evil and of the ethical commonwealth as the locus in which human moral agents are called upon to engage one another's freedom in concert for the overcoming of radical evil not just in its individual form of self-preference but also in the divisiveness in which such self-preference takes conflictual social form.

A further association that Kant's text suggests regarding the relation between politics and religion in the critical project is one that links together the key moral, political, and religious images and tropes he uses for the social empowerment of human freedom. The moral/religious trope of an ethical commonwealth, the political trope of a cosmopolitan world order, and the theological trope of the kingdom of God each serve as a marker of the active participation of human freedom that is requisite for the enactment of the highest good as the final end of reason. It is this last trope, moreover, with its inflection that is unmistakably both religious and political, that Kant sees as the center of the good news of liberation from subjection to the dominion of evil that Jesus proclaims. As Kant articulates this image, he construes the kingdom of God as an achievement that, even though it has been decisively inaugurated by Jesus, will require the participation of human agency, exercising its freedom, for its lasting establishment.[65] Just as the engagement of human freedom is required for the enactment of the social dynamic of full mutuality in the ethical commonwealth and for the functioning of the structures for maintaining peace among nations in a cosmopolitan world order, the enactment of the kingdom of God also requires the active and sustained historical engagement of human freedom.[66] Human freedom is required as the socially shaping dynamism for the mutual recognition and respect that overcome exclusivities and divisiveness in human social interaction, particularly those from which come the most violent and virulent forms of social conflict. Cosmopolitan hope for the efficacy of human participation in the establishment of an international order of peace among nations and the pure religious (moral) faith exhibited socially in the mutual recognition and respect constitutive of the ethical commonwealth converge

---

refusal of a courtier to accede to the prince's demand to perjure himself, the consciousness of the moral law that Kant terms "the fact of reason" (CPrR 5:30).

[65] Kant articulates this participation in terms of a transition from the "ecclesiastical faith" of merely outward observance to the "pure religious faith" of mutual respect in an ethical commonwealth (Rel. 6:115–124).

[66] W. Ertl's Element in this series, *Perpetual Peace: Metaphysical Foundations of Kant's Highest Political Good*, offers an illuminating overview of the issues bearing on the metaphysics of agency that are implicated in Kant's efforts to articulate how both human and divine freedom function together in effecting the highest good.

upon what Kant proposes, in two significant texts, as the categorical imperative of peace:

> [Y]et reason, from the throne of the highest morally legislative power, delivers an absolute condemnation of war as a procedure for determining rights and, on the contrary, makes a condition of peace, which cannot be instituted or assured without a pact of nations among themselves, a direct duty. (TPP 8:356)

> Now morally practical reason pronounces in us its irresistible *veto: there is to be no war*, neither war between you and me in the state of nature nor between us as states, which, although they are internally in a lawful condition, are still externally (in relation to one another) in a lawless condition; for war is not the way in which anyone should seek his rights. (MM 8:354)

Such convergence upon an imperative of and for peace suggests that each of these tropes points to yet another with scriptural roots: "the peaceable kingdom."

All these tropes provide a horizon of hope that offers space for human agency to have a genuine moral efficacy that, by overcoming divisiveness, participates in forming the highest good in a social inflection that serves in establishing conditions for peace. The horizon of hope framed by these images enables attainment of peace to be construed in social terms that require efficacy in the overcoming of divisiveness. Against this horizon, hope is most fundamentally a *social hope*, made possible by the dynamic of full mutuality that each image expresses in distinctive, but related ways. It is this perspective of social hope that will then provide the most encompassing basis for articulating the complementary functions played by Kant's political philosophy and his philosophy of religion in unfolding the anthropological trajectory of his critical project. That horizon, as noted at a number of points in this Element, is one that functions to enable the enactment of full mutual moral recognition as the constitutive dynamic of the all-embracing social contexts – world, commonwealth, and kingdom – that are figured in each of these images.

This perspective of social hope, moreover, takes one of the key bearings of its orientation in moral "counterpoint" to what is arguably the central point of Kant's often reiterated account of human moral failure: the self-preferential obduracy – the preference for "the dear self" – that goes "down deep" in the individual moral agency of us all.[67] Not only does such obduracy manifest itself as the radical evil disorienting human agency into a pattern of self-preference

---

[67] J. Mariña, "What Perfection Demands: An Irenaean Account of Kant on Radical Evil," in *Kant and the Question of Theology*, pp. 283–200, offers an insightful treatment of the dimensions of what I have termed human "moral obduracy."

that neglects the mutuality of respect constitutive of the social character of human finite freedom. It is central in fueling the divisiveness and contention that arises from "unsociable sociability" and that makes the social form of radical evil, war, possible.[68] On this basis, one could then argue that a core dynamic of the critical project arises from the recognition of the need for humanity to undertake, in full freedom, the intellectual and moral discipline, i.e., critique, that will enable us to counter such self-preferential obduracy in all its forms, individual and social – and most especially in its most virulent social manifestation, war.

In the context of this need to counter the self-preferential obduracy of our agency, the suggestion put forth here is that the horizon of hope provided by these images can be seen to function as a "grammar" for *the social instantiation of the recognition of our fundamental human mutuality that stands athwart the dynamics of self-preference*: this horizon provides the structure for a syntax of moral recognition that places a constraint upon both the explicit and implicit claims of self-preference that deflect, preclude, and undermine the effective acknowledgment of our human mutuality and its moral weight for both the individual and social exercise of our freedom.[69] Such a syntax of moral recognition is embedded in Kant's moral philosophy as a deep grammar for the appropriate exercise of human freedom. It can be found, for instance, in the formulations of the categorical imperative – e.g., universal law, of humanity as an end in itself – that place a veto of mutuality upon the self-preferential obduracy that urges upon individual moral agents a self-exemption from the universal requirements of moral reason.[70] It is also operative in the discourse of mutual respect appropriate to membership and shared responsibility in what Kant terms a kingdom of ends; such discourse helps to post reminders against the exemptions from mutuality that we are otherwise tempted make for

---

[68] An important text in which Kant employs the term "unsociable sociability" is the "Fourth Proposition" of "Idea for a Universal History with a Cosmopolitan Aim" (8: 20–22), where he describes it in the following terms: "Here I understand by 'antagonism' the *unsociable sociability* of human beings, i.e. their propensity to enter into society, which, however, is combined with a thoroughgoing resistance that constantly threatens to break up this society." He provides an important later commentary on "unsociable sociability" – without using that terminology – in the beginning of Part III of *Religion* (6:93–100). See A. W. Wood, "Unsociable Sociability: The Anthropological Basis of Kantian Ethics" *Philosophical Topics* 19:1 (Spring 1991): 325–351.

[69] Kant offers an extended exercise of such a "grammar" with respect to what one may and may not appropriately say of oneself morally with respect to "the possibility of realizing in us the idea of a humanity well pleasing to God" – i.e., about our own moral condition with respect to "the rightful claim of the good principle" upon us – in *Religion* Part II, Section 1, C (Rel. 6:66–78).

[70] Placing these formulations in the context of the self-preferential obduracy of radical evil suggests that their focus is more on the veto they impose on self-preference and self-exemption as stratagems that issue from "the dear self" than on a formal claim of "universalizability" that generations of Kant's critics have castigated as a moral version of "one size fits all." See Wood, *Kant's Ethical Thought*, chapters 3–5, pp. 76–190, for a thorough discussion.

ourselves. The tug of the dear self is also at work in the social dynamic that Kant terms unsociable sociability, which, even though it has power to draw us together, far more often conspires with our self-preferential obduracy to drive us asunder into hostile camps of "us" and "them."[71] Moral obduracy, working in concert with unsociable sociability, provides space not only for conflict among individuals' self-preferences but also for various social alliances to cloak their dynamics of fracture, factionalism, and power as simulacra of legitimate common interests.

In view of the limitations that moral obduracy and unsociable sociability can place upon the moral hope enabled by an individual agent's exercise of moral freedom, the enlarged social horizon of hope that a cosmopolitan world order and the ethical commonwealth bring to human efforts to attain the highest good take on great importance. Our individual exercise of practical reason does provide us with a moral faith, enabling hope for our steadfastness in ordering our maxims in accord with the full scope of reason's moral demand, yet it does not license a moral presumptuousness that one will, *in fact*, always heed that demand.[72] Neither does it thereby unproblematically permit immediate extension of that hope *to the agency of others*. Such hope seems confined to a perspective upon one's individual moral constancy that does not explicitly attend to the mutuality that shapes our moral agency, or to the individual and social obstacles we help to place in its path. Over against an awareness of the moral obduracy captured in the image of the "crooked wood" of our humanity, such individually focused hope is hard won and often fragile.[73] To the extent that one frames and adopts such maxims according to the universal scope of reason's moral demand, one may hope to stand resolutely against one's own self-preferential obduracy: awareness that "I can" gives hope that "I will" – yet even that does not *guarantee* actual performance in all instances; nor does it seem sufficient to overcome by itself the social forms of the obduracy of self-preference that foster divisiveness and fuel social conflict.

In consequence, such an individually focused horizon of hope seems hardly strong enough to provide a basis for a robust social extension of that hope to others: we are *all* equally prone to such self-preferential warping into crooked wood; that proclivity, moreover, may be intensified all the more as our obduracy of self-preference seeks out alliance with others under the dynamics of

---

[71] Kant uses the expression "the dear self" in *Groundwork of the Metaphysics of Morals* (4:407).

[72] Though "I ought" implies "I can," it does not, for Kant, thereby imply "I will." On this, Kant would side with Augustine over against Socrates: knowing the good is not sufficient to empower us to do the good.

[73] Two of Kant's notable uses of the image of "crooked wood" are "For from such crooked wood as man is made of, nothing perfectly straight can be built" (IUH 8:23) and "But how should one expect to construct something completely straight from such crooked wood?" (Rel. 6:100).

unsociable sociability.[74] In the context of our unsociable sociability, hope has an even more urgent need to extend its scope beyond what moral agents may hope for themselves individually as the outcome of their right conduct. It needs to orient us more fully upon those coordinates that enable our recognition of the depth of the mutuality in which our conduct and its outcome are embedded. That recognition is one that, on Kant's account, emerges from the capacity of self-governing moral agents to acknowledge and engage one another in mutuality, as equal participants in the modalities of social hope envisioned in each of these images: in the ordering of mutuality as a "kingdom of ends" that is constitutive of an ethical commonwealth; in the construction of the practices and institutions for the establishment of cosmopolitan order of international peace; in extending the moral reach of the kingdom of God; or, as Kant's idiom from earlier texts would express it, as co-legislators for a kingdom of ends.

This larger social context is the one envisioned in Kant's three images of an ethical commonwealth, a cosmopolitan world order of peace, and the kingdom of God. They provide bases for a syntax of moral recognition that functions to clear a social space within which agents address not only questions of individual human interaction but also those pertaining to the larger sphere of the social governance of human life.[75] On Kant's account, a grammar of social hope functions on a scale even larger than the important one of breaking the grip of self-preferential obduracy with respect to the moral life of individual moral agents. It also extends into workings of the dynamics by which reason empowers human agents to govern their social, political, and cultural interaction with one another in accord with an inclusive mutuality that breaks the social grip of the self-preferential obduracy at work in unsocial sociability. Hope in this latter context is thus concerned not so much with what one's own moral power may bring about in the face of the internal tug from one's own self-regarding maxims, but with what may be effected *in concert with the moral power of others* in the face of the power of unsociable sociability to reinforce the self-preferential obduracy that would drive us apart into factions and set the dynamics of conflict in motion.

In this instance, the question of hope bears not just upon the moral destiny of the individual as it might be figured religiously, for instance in Christianity

---

[74] See P. J. Rossi, "The Crooked Wood of Human History: The Ethical Commonwealth and the Persistence of Evil," in *Natur und Freiheit: Akten des XII. Internationalen Kant-Kongresses*. Band 4, ed. V. Waibel, M. Ruffing, and D. Wagner, with S. Gerber (Berlin: W. de Gruyter, 2018), pp. 2591–2598.

[75] J. Rawls's device of "the original position" in *A Theory of Justice* (Cambridge, MA: Belknap Press of Harvard University Press, 1971) from which (ideal) agents deliberate on equal terms with one another about the terms of their social governance captures an important dimension of the social space of mutuality that is a function of a syntax of mutual recognition.

as well as other religions, as a form of "everlasting life." In the context of the social character embedded in the tropes that Kant employs to articulate the shape of the good to be enacted in humanity's moral vocation, the question of hope also bears upon larger and more challenging outcomes for humanity as a whole and for the cosmos of which humanity is a part. One of these outcomes is envisioned as the project of establishing the conditions for an international order of peace, for which the establishment of an order of "cosmopolitan hospitality" provides an important marker;[76] another, similarly large in scope, and of increasing urgency in the face of the scale and scope of environmental degradation in this age, is a restructuring of the engagement of human freedom with nature in the biosphere to turn it away from a destructive dynamic of consumption toward one that manifests the respect appropriate to humanity's vocation to be the juncture of nature and freedom.[77]

These outcomes are ones that, on Kant's account of humanity's moral vocation, need to be envisioned as ensuing in history and society in consequence of human enactment – or failure of enactment – of the social accountability we owe one another in virtue of our fundamental mutuality as members of an ethical commonwealth and a cosmopolitan world order. They are functions of the attainment of the good that constitutes a common and shared destiny for all humanity and indeed for the entire cosmos. In view of the inclusive social scope of these outcomes, hope requires us to consider the extent to which the exercise of our moral reason also requires us to enact for one another practices and conditions enabling us to place confidence in the proper exercise of *one another's* moral autonomy in respectful mutuality even as we stand aware of the moral opacity that allows us to conceal our own self-preferential moral obduracy not only from ourselves individually but also from one another.[78]

---

[76] Kant places the articulation of cosmopolitan hospitality as a right to visit in the context of trade and commerce (TPP 8:357–360; MM 6:351–352), while at the same time providing a brief but quite acerbic critique of colonial exploitation and expropriation. It might be instructive to speculate what Kant might propose regarding hospitality in our early twenty-first-century circumstances in which widespread and, in some cases, long-term displacement of peoples looms as an intensifying humanitarian crisis.

[77] A recent scientific and culturally inflected reminder of how human and cosmic destiny are closely intertwined is pertinent here. This is the debate vigorously under way among geologists and environmental scientists about the appropriateness of designating the current terrestrial epoch as the "anthropocene" in view of the impact human activity has had upon the global environment. See J. Stromberg, "What Is the Anthropocene and Are We Living in It?" (*Smithsonian Magazine*, January 2013). www.smithsonianmag.com/science-nature/what-is-the-anthropocene-and-are-we-in-it-164801414/ (accessed July 5, 2018).

[78] J. Rawls's other device in *A Theory of Justice*, "a veil of ignorance," is well attuned to the issue of establishing mutual trust among agents aware of the structural dynamics of self-preference and self-opacity in their agency.

This suggests what may, in the end, be of the most fundamental import for the role that Kant sees for religion with respect to the attainment of the highest good possible in the world; it bears upon our capacity for seeing that good as *a social good for which we have the capacity for effecting in concert with one another*. Kant, unsurprisingly, considers the efficacy of human freedom as a participant in attaining good as requisite for it to be an authentically human moral good. The social horizon that the ethical commonwealth – along with the other tropes – provides upon the efficacy of the human enactment of good makes it also requisite that such enactment be fully attentive to the nexus of relationality out of which it comes and on which it acts. In other words, we must be attentive, as we envision ourselves as participants in the social dynamics of the mutuality proposed to us in each of these tropes, to the *thoroughly social* character of what we seek to enact and of its interrelatedness to the social manner of its enactment.

A central mark of this social good is its power to overcome dynamics of human divisiveness that arise from the moral obduracy of both individual and social forms of self-preference. On Kant's account, critically disciplined religion orients itself toward the universal horizon that reason provides for engaging the freedom of human moral agents in the dynamics of the mutual recognition and respect that overcome self-preference. This horizon enables the establishment, in full social form, of the dynamics of human recognition and respect that Kant terms the ethical commonwealth. This horizon, moreover, also encompasses the construction of a cosmopolitan order for the attainment of international peace. Kant envisions this order *as a necessary external mark of the full social form of the inclusive mutual recognition and respect* that, in the ethical commonwealth, is instantiated as the constant inner orientation of the moral freedom of human agency to full and inclusive mutual recognition.

Kant thus envisions both critically disciplined religion in the form of an ethical commonwealth and a cosmopolitan world order as each empowering the exercise of human freedom to enact social dynamics that overcome division and conflict and to create conditions for a "peaceable kingdom." They do so by their complementary orientation to a horizon of mutual recognition and respect. This orientation is enacted in and by the ethical commonwealth, which offers a concrete instantiation of the practice of authentic religion by being the lived and living social expression of the dynamics of inclusive mutual respect. As such an instantiation, it provides a model of full human mutuality, inviting all to orient their lives to the horizon of inclusivity and universality expressed in the trope of the kingdom of God, as well as in the moral/political trope of a cosmopolitan world order. This model, in accord with Jesus's mode of living, is formed in social dynamics of inclusive mutual respect; it makes possible the overcoming of exclusivities and divisiveness in human social interaction, particularly those exclusivities from which the most violent and virulent form of social conflict, war, emerges. In this role, religion as a locus empowering the social exercise of human freedom to enact possibilities for overcoming division and conflict stands in religious complementary to the political empowerment that a cosmopolitan perspective provides for the conditions and social structures that foster the attainment of perpetual peace.

Bibliography

A Note on Translation and Citations to the Works of Kant

Citations to the *Critique of Pure Reason* use the standard convention of reference, A/B, in which A corresponds to the pagination of the first (1781) edition, and B corresponds to the pagination of the second (1787) edition. Citations to the other works of Kant are referenced to the pagination of the *Akademie Augabe* (AA), the critical edition of Kant's collected works (*Immanuel Kants Schriften*, Ausgabe der königlich preussischen Akademie der Wissenschaften [Berlin: W. de Gruyter, 1902–]), followed by the volume and page number – e.g., CPrR 5:3–4.

The works of Kant quoted and referenced in the text of this Element are listed in what follows with their German titles, in the chronological order of their original publication, and referenced by the notation "AA" to the volume in which they appear in the critical edition, *Immanuel Kants Schriften*, Ausgabe der königlich preussischen Akademie der Wissenschaften (Berlin: W. de Gruyter, 1902–). These are followed by the notation "Cam" followed by the title of the English translation published in *The Cambridge Edition of the Works of Immanuel Kant*, Paul Guyer and Allen Wood, general editors (Cambridge: Cambridge University Press, 1993–2012), the name of the translator, and the title of the volume in the series in which it appears.

CPR   *Kritik der reinen Vernunft*, 1781; 2nd edition 1787 (AA 3–4). Cam: *Critique of Pure Reason*, translated by Paul Guyer and Allen W. Wood, 1998.

P   *Prolegomena zu einer jeden künftigen Metaphysik, die als Wissenschaft wird auftreten können*, 1783 (AA 4). Cam: *Prolegomena to Any Future Metaphysics That Will Be Able to Come Forward as Science*, translated by Gary Hatfield and Michael Freidman, in *Theoretical Philosophy after 1781*, 2002, pp. 49–169.

IUH   "Idee zu einer allgemeinen Geschichte in weltbürgerlichen Absicht," 1784 (AA 8: 15–31). Cam: "Idea for a Universal History with a Cosmopolitan Aim," translated by Allen W. Wood, in *Anthropology, History, and Education*, 2007, pp. 107–120.

WIE   "Beantwortung der Frage: Was ist Aufklärung?" 1784 (AA 8:33–42). Cam: "An Answer to the Question: What Is Enlightenment?" translated by Mary J. Gregor, in *Practical Philosophy*, 1996, pp. 17–22.

G   *Grundlegung zur Metaphysik der Sitten*, 1785 (AA 4: 385–463). Cam: *Groundwork of the Metaphysics of Morals*, translated by Mary J. Gregor, in *Practical Philosophy*, 1996, pp. 43–108.

MFNS   *Metaphysische Anfangsgründe der Naturwissenschaft* 1786 (AA 4). Cam: *Metaphysical Foundations of Natural Science*, translated by Michael Friedman, in *Theoretical Philosophy after 1781*, 2002, pp. 183–270.

WOT   "Was heisst: Sich im Denken orientieren?" 1786 (AA 8:131–147). Cam: "What Does It Mean to Orient Oneself in Thinking?" translated by Allen W. Wood, in *Religion and Rational Theology*, 1996, pp. 7–18.

CPrR   *Kritik der praktischen Vernunft*, 1788 (AA 5: 1–163). Cam: *Critique of Practical Reason*, translated by Mary J. Gregor, in *Practical Philosophy*, 1996, pp. 139–271.

TP   "Über den Gemeinspruch: Das Mag in der Theorie richtig sein, taugt aber nicht für die Praxis," 1793 (AA 8:273–313). Cam: "On the Common Saying: That May Be Correct in Theory But It Is of No Use in Practice," translated by Mary J. Gregor, in *Practical Philosophy*, 1996, pp. 279–309.

Rel.   *Die Religion innerhalb der Grenzen der blossen Vernunft*, 1793 (AA 6: 1–202). Cam: *Religion within the Boundaries of Mere Reason*, translated by George Di Giovanni, in *Religion and Rational Theology*, 1996, pp. 37–215.

TPP   "Zum ewigen Frieden: Ein philosophischer Entwurf," 1795 (AA 8:341–386). Cam: "Toward Perpetual Peace," translated by Mary J. Gregor, in *Practical Philosophy*, 1996, pp. 317–351.

MM   *Metaphysik der Sitten: 1. Metaphysische Anfangsgründe der Rechtslehre, 2. Metaphysiche Anfangsgründe der Tugendlehre*, 1797 (AA 6:203–493). Cam: *The Metaphysics of Morals*, translated by Mary J. Gregor, in *Practical Philosophy*, 1996, pp. 365–603.

CF   *Der Streit der Fakultäten*: Erneuerte Frage: Ob das menschliche Geschlecht im beständigen Fortschreiten zum Besseren sei, 1798 (AA 7:1–116). Cam: *The Conflict of the Faculties*: "An Old Question Raised Again: Is the Human Race Constantly Progressing?" translated by Mary J. Gregor and Robert Anchor, in *Religion and Rational Theology*, 1996, pp. 239–327.

Corr.   *Briefwechsel* I–III (AA 10–12). Cam: *Correspondence*, translated by Arnulf Zweig, 1999.

JL   *Jäsche Logic*, AA 9: 1–150; Cam: *Lectures on Logic*, translated by J. Michael Young, 1992, pp. 519–640.

Books

Anderson-Gold, S., *Unnecessary Evil: History and Moral Progress in the Philosophy of Immanuel Kant*, Albany: State University of New York Press, 2001.

Arendt, H., *Lectures on Kant's Political Philosophy: Edited with an Interpretive Essay by Ronald Beiner*, Chicago: University of Chicago Press, 1982.

Cavallar, G., *Kant's Embedded Cosmopolitanism: History, Philosophy and Education for World Citizens*, Kantstudien-Ergänzungshefte 183, Berlin, Boston: W. de Gruyter, 2015.

Collins, J., *A History of Modern European Philosophy*, Milwaukee, WI: Bruce Publishing, 1954.

The Emergence of Philosophy of Religion, New Haven, CT: Yale University Press, 1967.

Despland, M., *Kant on History and Religion*, Montreal: McGill-Queen's University Press, 1973.

Ertl, W., *Perpetual Peace: Metaphysical Foundations of Kant's Highest Political Good*, Cambridge: Cambridge University Press, forthcoming.

Firestone, C. L., Jacobs, N. A., and Joiner, J. H., eds., *Kant and the Question of Theology*, Cambridge: Cambridge University Press, 2017.

Fischer, N., ed., *Kant und der Katholizismus. Stationen einer wechselhaften Geschichte*, Freiburg: Verlag Herder, 2005.

Goldmann, L., *Immanuel Kant*, trans. Robert Black, London: NLB, 1971. German: *Mensch, Gemeinschaft und Welt in der Philosophie Immanuel Kants*, Zurich: Europa Verlag, 1945.

Hume, D., *A Treatise of Human Nature* (1738–1740), ed. L. A. Selby-Bigge, Oxford: Clarendon Press, 1888, rpt. 1968.

Insole, C. J., *The Intolerable God: Kant's Theological Journey*, Grand Rapids, MI: William B. Eerdmans, 2016.

Kleingeld, P., *Kant and Cosmopolitanism: The Philosophical Ideal of World Citizenship*, Cambridge: Cambridge University Press, 2012.

Louden, R., *Kant's Impure Ethics: From Rational Beings to Human Beings*, New York: Oxford University Press, 2000.

Michalson Jr., G. E., *Fallen Freedom: Kant on Radical Evil and Moral Regeneration*, Cambridge: Cambridge University Press, 1990.

Kant and the Problem of God, Oxford: Blackwell, 1999.

Neiman, S., *The Unity of Reason: Re-reading Kant*, Oxford: Oxford University Press, 1994.

Evil in Modern Thought: An Alternative History of Philosophy, Princeton, NJ: Princeton University Press, 2002.

O'Neill, O., *Constructions of Reason*, Cambridge: Cambridge University Press, 1989.

Palmquist, S. R., *Comprehensive Commentary on Kant's Religion within the Bounds of Bare Reason*, Chichester: Wiley, 2016.

Pasternack, L. R., *Kant on Religion within the Boundaries of Mere Reason*, London: Routledge, 2014.

Rawls, J., *A Theory of Justice*, Cambridge, MA: Belknap Press of Harvard University Press, 1971.

Riley, P., *Kant's Political Philosophy*, Totowa, NJ: Rowman & Allanheld, 1983.

Rossi, P. J., *The Social Authority of Reason: Kant's Critique, Radical Evil and the Destiny of Humankind*, Albany: State University of New York Press, 2005.

Williams, H., *Kant's Political Philosophy*, Oxford: Basil Blackwell, 1983.

Kant and the End of War: A Critique of Just War Theory, New York: Palgrave Macmillan, 2012.

Wilson, H. L., *Kant's Pragmatic Anthropology: Its Origin, Meaning, and Critical Significance*, Albany: State University of New York Press, 2006.

Wood, A. W., *Kant's Moral Religion*, Ithaca, NY: Cornell University Press, 1970.

Kant's Ethical Thought, Cambridge: Cambridge University Press, 1999.

Zammito, J. H., *Kant, Herder, and the Birth of Anthropology*, Chicago: University of Chicago Press, 2002.

Journal Articles and Book Chapters

Abraham, W. J., "Divine Agency and Divine Action in Immanuel Kant," in *Kant and the Question of Theology*, ed. C. L. Firestone, N. A. Jacobs, and J. H. Joiner, Cambridge: Cambridge University Press, 2017: 138–158.

Adams, R. M., "Introduction," in *Religion within the Boundaries of Mere Reason and Other Writings*, Cambridge Texts in the History of Philosophy, Cambridge: Cambridge University Press, 1998: xxxv–xxxvii.

Beiser, F. C., "Moral Faith and the Highest Good," in *The Cambridge Companion to Kant and Modern Philosophy*, ed. P. Guyer, Cambridge: Cambridge University Press, 2006: 588–629.

Firestone, C. L. and S. R. Palmquist, "Editor's Introduction," in *Kant and the New Philosophy of Religion*, Bloomington: Indiana University Press, 2006: 1–39.

Mariña, J., "What Perfection Demands: An Irenaean Account of Kant on Radical Evil," in *Kant and the Question of Theology*, ed. C. L. Firestone, N. A. Jacobs, and J. H. Joiner, Cambridge: Cambridge University Press, 2017: 283–300.

Mertens, T., "Kant and the Just War Tradition," in *From Just War to Modern Peace Ethics*, ed. W. A. Barbieri Jr. and H.-G. Justenhoven, Berlin: W. de Gruyter, 2012: 231–247.

Neiman, S., "Meaning and Metaphysics," in *Teaching New Histories of Philosophy*, ed. J. B. Schneewind, Princeton, NJ: University Center for Human Values, 2004: 29–50.

O'Neill, O., "Reason and Politics in the Kantian Enterprise," in *Constructions of Reason: Explorations of Kant's Practical Philosophy*, Cambridge: Cambridge University Press, 1989: 3–27.

"Enactable and Enforceable: Kant's Criteria for Right and Virtue," *Kant-Studien* 107 (2016): 111–124.

Rossi, P. J., "The Crooked Wood of Human History: The Ethical Commonwealth and the Persistence of Evil," in *Natur und Freiheit: Akten des XII. Internationalen Kant-Kongresses*. Band 4, ed. V. Waibel, M. Ruffing, D. Wagner, with S. Gerber. Berlin: W. de Gruyter, 2018: 2591–2598.

"War as Morally Unintelligible: Sovereign Agency and the Limits of Kantian Autonomy," *The Monist* 99:1 (2016): 1–12. doi:10.1093/monist/onv025. http://monist.oxfordjournals.org/content/monist/99/1/1.full.pdf?ijkey=AhLgRM5nOaxtVrs&keytype=ref

"Peacemaking and Victory: Lessons from Kant's Cosmopolitanism," *Philosophia: Philosophical Quarterly of Israel* 43:3 (2015): 747–757. http://link.springer.com/article/10.1007/s11406-015-9615-5

"Expanding the Horizon of Kant's Ethics: Recent Interpretations of the Foundations of the Metaphysics of Morals," *Chiedza: Journal of Arrupe College* (Harare) 17:1 (2014): 74–86.

"Cosmopolitanism: Kant's Social Anthropology of Hope," in *Kant und die Philosophie in weltbürgerlicher Absicht: Akten des XI. Kant-Kongresses 2010*, ed. S. Bacin, A. Ferrarin, C. La Rocca, and M. Ruffing, Berlin: W. de Gruyter, 2013, Bd. 4: 827–837.

"Kant's Apophaticism of Finitude: A Grammar of Hope for Speaking Humanly of God," *The Linguistic Dimension of Kant's Thought: Historical and Critical Essays*, ed. F. Schalow and R. Velkley, Evanston, IL: Northwestern University Press, 2014: 154–173.

"Kant's Cosmopolitanism: Resource for Shaping a 'Just Peace'," in *From Just War to Modern Peace Ethics*, ed. H. G. Justenhoven and W. A. Barbieri, Berlin: W. de Gruyter, 2012: 217–230.

"Models of God and Just War Theory," in *Models of God and Alternative Ultimate Realities*, ed. A. Kasher and J. Diller, Dordrecht: Springer Verlag, 2013: 991–1000.

"Reading Kant from a Catholic Horizon: Ethics and the Anthropology of Grace," *Theological Studies* 71 (2010): 79–100.

"War: The Social Form of Radical Evil," in *Kant und die Berliner Aufklärung: Akten des IX. Internationalen Kant-Kongresses*, Band 4, ed. V. Gerhardt, R.-P. Horstmann, and R. Schumacher, Berlin: W. de Gruyter, 2001: 248–256.

Stromberg, J., "What Is the Anthropocene and Are We Living in It?" *Smithsonian Magazine*, January 2013. www.smithsonianmag.com/science-nature/what-is-the-anthropocene-and-are-we-in-it-164801414/ (accessed July 22, 2018).

Walsh, W. H., "Kant," in *The Encyclopedia of Philosophy*, ed. P. Edwards, New York: Macmillan Publishing & The Free Press, 1967, 3:305–324.

Williams, H., "Metaphysical and not just Political," in *Politics and Metaphysics in Kant*, ed. H. Williams, S. Pihlström, and S. Baiasu, Cardiff: University of Wales Press, 2011: 215–232.

Wood, A. W. "Unsociable Sociability: The Anthropological Basis of Kantian Ethics," *Philosophical Topics* 19:1 (Spring 1991): 325–351.

"The Final Form of Kant's Practical Philosophy," *Southern Journal of Philosophy* 36:S1 (1997): 1–20.

Cambridge Elements ⌶

The Philosophy of Immanuel Kant

Desmond Hogan
Princeton University
Desmond Hogan joined the philosophy department at Princeton in 2004. His interests include Kant, Leibniz and German rationalism, early modern philosophy, and questions about causation and freedom. Recent work includes Kant on Foreknowledge of Contingent Truths, *Res Philosophica* 91 (1) (2014); 'Kant's Theory of Divine and Secondary Causation', in Brandon Look (ed.) *Leibniz and Kant*, Oxford University Press (forthcoming); 'Kant and the Character of Mathematical Inference', in *Kant's Philosophy of Mathematics Vol. I*, Carl Posy and Ofra Rechter (eds.), Cambridge University Press (2019).

Howard Williams
University of Cardiff
Howard Williams was appointed Honorary Distinguished Professor at the Department of Politics and International Relations, University of Cardiff in 2014. He is also Emeritus Professor in Political Theory at the Department of International Politics, Aberystwyth University, a member of the Coleg Cymraeg Cenedlaethol (Welsh-language national college) and a Fellow of the Learned Society of Wales. He is the author of *Marx* (1980); *Kant's Political Philosophy* (1983); *Concepts of Ideology* (1988); *International Relations in Political Theory* (1992); *Hegel, Heraclitus and Marx's Dialectic; International Relations and the Limits of Political Theory* (1996); *Kant's Critique of Hobbes: Sovereignty and Cosmopolitanism* (2003), *Kant and the End of War* (2012) and is currently editor of the journal *Kantian Review*. He is writing a book on the Kantian legacy in political philosophy for a new series edited by Paul Guyer.

Allen Wood
Indiana University
Allen Wood is Ward W. and Pricilla B. Woods Professor at Stanford University. He was a John S. Guggenheim Fellow at the Free University in Berlin, a national Endowment for the Humanities Fellow at the University of Bonn and Isaiah Berlin Visiting Professor at the University of Oxford. He is on the editorial board of eight philosophy journals, five book series and the *Stanford Encyclopedia of Philosophy*. Along with Paul Guyer, Professor Wood is co-editor of the *Cambridge Edition of the Works of Immanuel Kant* and translator of the *Critique of Pure Reason*. He is the author or editor of a number of other works, mainly on Kant, Hegel and Karl Marx. His most recently published book, *Fichte's Ethical Thought*, was published by Oxford University Press in 2016. Wood is a member of the American Academy of Arts and Sciences.

About the Series

This Cambridge Elements series provides an extensive overview of Kant's philosophy and its impact upon philosophy and philosophers. Distinguished Kant specialists will provide an up-to-date summary of the results of current research in their fields and give their own take on what they believe are the most significant debates influencing research, drawing original conclusions.

Cambridge Elements ☰

The Philosophy of Immanuel Kant

Elements in the Series

Formulas of the Moral Law
Allen Wood

The Sublime
Melissa McBay Merritt

Kant's Power of Imagination
Rolf-Peter Horstmann

Kant on Civil Society and Welfare
Sarah Holtman

*The Ethical Commonwealth in History: Peace-Making
as the Moral Vocation of Humanity*
Philip J. Rossi

A full series listing is available at: www.cambridge.org/EPIK

Printed in the United States
By Bookmasters